Vladimir Krajina

WORLD WAR II HERO AND
ECOLOGY PIONEER

OTHER BOOKS BY
JAN DRABEK

~

IN ENGLISH:

Blackboard Odyssey (non-fiction, 1973)

Whatever Happened to Wenceslas? (fiction, 1973)

Melvin the Weather Moose (children's, 1976)

Report on the Death of Rosenkavalier (fiction, 1977)

The Lister Legacy (fiction, 1980)

The Statement (fiction, 1982)

The Golden Revolution (non-fiction, 1989)

The Exotic Canadians (fiction, 1990)

Thirteen (non-fiction, 1991)

I Luff You B.C. (non-fiction, 2001)

Grungia (fiction, 2012)

IN CZECH:

Náhle českým velvyslancem (fiction, 1997)

Po uši v postkomunismu (non-fiction, 2000)

Po uši v protektorátu (non-fiction, 2001)

Po uši v Americe (non-fiction, 2003)

Hledání štěstí u cizáků (non-fiction, 2005)

Miluji Tě, Britská Kolumbie (non-fiction, 2009)

Vladimir
KRAJINA

WORLD WAR II HERO AND ECOLOGY PIONEER

JAN DRABEK

RONSDALE

RONSDALE PRESS
3350 West 21st Avenue
Vancouver, B.C. Canada V6S 1G7
www.ronsdalepress.com

Typesetting: Julie Cochrane, in Granjon 11.5 pt on 15
Cover Design: Julie Cochrane
Front Cover Photos: Forest of Giants; Parade of Nazi Soldiers, c. 1940
Page vi Photo: Vladimir Krajina in his laboratory at UBC, c. 1958.
Paper: Ancient Forest Friendly Rolland Enviro Satin FSC Recycled —
    100% post-consumer waste, totally chlorine-free and acid-free.

Ronsdale Press wishes to thank the following for their support of its publishing program: the Canada Council for the Arts, the Government of Canada through the Canada Book Fund, the British Columbia Arts Council, and the Province of British Columbia through the British Columbia Book Publishing Tax Credit program.

Library and Archives Canada Cataloguing in Publication

Drábek, Jan, 1935–
    Vladimir Krajina: World War II hero and ecology pioneer / Jan Drabek.

Includes bibliographical references and index.
Issued also in electronic format.
ISBN 978-1-55380-147-4

    1. Krajina, V. J. (Vladimir Joseph), 1905–1993. 2. Botanists — Canada — Biography. 3. World War, 1939–1945 — Underground movements — Czechoslovakia — Biography. 4. Czech Canadians — Biography. 5. Ecological reserves — Canada — History. I. Title.

QK31.K7D73 2012   580.92   C2012-902663-8

At Ronsdale Press we are committed to protecting the environment. To this end we are working with Canopy (formerly Markets Initiative) and printers to phase out our use of paper produced from ancient forests. This book is one step towards that goal.

Printed in Canada by Marquis Book Printing, Quebec

CONTENTS

Introduction

DURING THE WAR *Krajina* was a just a concept. At least for me, initially. And not a very clear one at that. With a small "k" the word in Czech can mean the countryside. With a capital "K" it is a person's name. Since it's impossible to detect capitals in spoken language, I became thoroughly confused. Moreover, as a person, Krajina is masculine, as a landscape it's feminine, and around our family table it could be used interchangeably. Since I was seven at the time I was not too swift in grasping which was which; my brain merely registered the existence of some vague entity by that name. Somewhere.

It didn't help much that there was another entity bandied around the family dinner table at that time called *Drtina*. With a small "d," it means a material which has been crushed. But as is the case with Krajina, Drtina could also be a person's name. These mysteries were not explained by my parents: I think it was presumed that the greater the confusion in the minds of their progeny, the less likely my brother and I were to talk about either Krajina or Drtina at school.

When I first began hearing of these confusing entities, Krajina was either hiding from the Gestapo or being imprisoned by it. Drtina was permanently in a London exile, broadcasting weekly commentaries in Czech over the BBC, invariably predicting a sad end for the Third Reich. Both Krajina and Drtina, now fully materialized, are pictured alongside my father and two other prominent Resistance members on an oft-reproduced photograph as they met at a Prague airport in May 1945. Drtina was being welcomed from his London exile. For added piquancy, in the background there is a tank with some boisterous Red Army types on it — an ominous sign of things to come.

Slowly I began to understand that the "landscape" my parents referred to during the war was in fact this man with a dark mane which extended in a triangular fashion into his forehead. One of my father's best friends, though at that time he seemed seldom to smile, Vladimir Krajina was always kind to me. As I grew older I realized he was a great national hero who during the war had provided the Allies with valuable strategic information.

Along with his wife Marie (always referred to in our family as Mánička) and their daughter Milena, Krajina took up residence after the war two floors below in our apartment house. Milena was my exact contemporary. She not only attended the same school but was also in the same class. To complete the Krajina family group, there was a perennially smiling grandmother, Marie's mother.

It has become morbidly fashionable in today's Czech Republic to downplay the role of its wartime underground. Perhaps it did not produce such spectacularly colourful personalities as the Norwegian Max Manus or the Yugoslav Tito, but there were some sound reasons for this.

In wartime, there were over 1,000 kilometres of mostly hostile and mountainous terrain between Berlin and Belgrade, while the Norwegians, though Nazi-occupied, were mercifully separated from Hitler by an ocean. On the other hand the distance between Prague and Berlin is a mere 280 kilometres and over excellent roads. This is why it was so much easier for the Nazis to keep sabotage and partisan activity at a minimum in the Czech Protectorate. However, they were far less successful in controlling intelligence leaks, and this is where the Czech underground was second to none.

Also, the Norwegian underground came into existence only after the Nazi invasion of April 1940; the Yugoslavian even a year later. By that time, having been active for more than two years, the Czech underground had provided spectacular services for the Allies. Of course, also during that time many of its members had been imprisoned and executed.

The Norwegian resistance hero Manus, too, was being hunted, but periodically he was able to take a breather in neighbouring neutral Sweden, where he relaxed and sipped coffee or something stronger with the MI5 types at the British Embassy. And Tito was surrounded by his fellow partisans in territory effectively controlled by them. He was also supplied fairly regularly via air and sea by the British.

Nothing like that was available to Krajina. By comparison, for nearly two years between 1941 and 1943, with the Gestapo relentlessly hunting him down, Vladimir Krajina was mostly alone, being hidden by good people who risked their lives by providing him with shelter. One can imagine the effect such tension would have had on a man with lesser conviction and determination. Krajina not only survived but also managed, most of the time, to make sure his radio messages reached the Allies.

In touch with a highly placed Nazi official during those two years, Krajina and his group sent radio messages to London about such incidents as Hitler's cancellation of his plans for the invasion of Britain, the date of the planned Nazi attack in the Balkans and — perhaps most important of all — the date of Hitler's invasion of the USSR. Churchill duly informed Stalin but the Soviet dictator, true to form, distrusted any such news emanating from the West. He made no preparations, which cost the Soviet Union several thousand lives initially, millions in the long run.

For four years during the war, Krajina was either on the run or engaged in a dangerous chess game with the Gestapo. On every move depended the lives of many people. It was utterly exhausting both physically and mentally, yet nothing could thwart his determination. Even the Allied victory in 1945 did not bring the relaxation and complete return to his beloved botany which he craved so much. There was now a new enemy in the form of yet another madman. This time his name was Stalin.

This writer remembers a group of Czech wartime Resistance workers meeting in their New York City exile during the 1950s. Somehow the conversation turned to the 1942 film *Casablanca*, which featured a supposed leader of the Czechoslovak wartime underground with the Hungarian name of Victor Laszlo. It was played by Paul Henreid, a refugee from Austrian Nazism.

To a man they had loved the movie, although not as a documentary but as a well-acted fairytale. To start off, the idea that Laszlo, the most sought-after escapee from the Nazis, could be walking about in Nazi-controlled Casablanca in a well-ironed white suit while sipping champagne cocktails at Rick's Café Americain may have appealed to the Hollywood mogul Jack Warner, but would have certainly been inconsistent with the actions of a genuine conspirator. By contrast, Krajina, the true Czech underground leader, adopted a different name and grew a beard before he ventured out in public in the remote Czech Paradise area.

In the film there is a scene in which the Vichy police break up an underground meeting and Laszlo escapes with the head waiter from the café explaining that "the police broke up our meeting, we escaped in the last moment." When detecting such meetings in the Czech lands, the Nazis always made sure that such meeting places were completely surrounded. Moreover, Krajina never attended such gatherings, preferring walks through dark streets and, if possible, a one-on-one arrangement.

Perhaps least believable in the film is the incessant clever banter among the Gestapo Major Strasser (who for some reason wears a dress *Luftwaffe* uniform), the police chief, Rick and Laszlo. Strasser bargains with Laszlo, and when Laszlo refuses to divulge the names of underground leaders throughout Europe, he informs him that "it is my duty that you stay in Casablanca." In reality it would have been his duty either to take him back to Germany or have him shot.

On the subject of the European underground leaders in Paris, Athens, Amsterdam and even Berlin, it's significant to note that Krajina always did his best not to know anyone beyond the closest group of conspirators precisely for that reason: so that under torture he could not have betrayed them. Also, the Nazis kept an air-tight control on communications between the various parts of their empire because the emergence of anything resembling an underground network would have spelled an end to their designs on controlling Europe.

And when Laszlo tells Strasser that even giving him the names of the leaders would not help the Germans because "from every corner hundreds, thousands would rise in our place" — and these people the Germans would be unable to kill — he is unfortunately sadly mistaken. As Krajina saw after the assassination of the SS leader Heydrich, the subsequent murderous rampage of the Nazis prevented the underground from ever again repeating its major successes.

And speaking of the Heydrich assassination, just how naïvely the Americans initially saw the European Resistance is evident in a 1943 Hollywood film called *Hangmen Also Die*. In it, after letting a group of students go without checking a single identity, a Prague university professor is arrested by the Gestapo and he asks: "On what charge?"

Had he seen the film, Krajina, who saw many a bloodied body brought to the Gestapo headquarters when he was incarcerated there, would probably have produced a sad smile. Especially after Heydrich's death, those arrested wouldn't have dared to ask anything. The standard procedure was to stand quietly facing the wall while the Gestapo thoroughly ransacked your apartment.

But there is one scene in *Casablanca* with which not only Krajina but quite likely every Resistance member would agree was authentic. It comes when Rick, while bandaging Laszlo's injured hand, asks if he had ever wondered if it's worth all this: "You might as well question why we breathe. If we stop breathing, we will die. If we stop fighting our enemies, the world will die."

In a way Vladimir Krajina's career was reminiscent of a Walt Disney character in his prize-winning 1938 film, *Ferdinand the Bull*. It tells of a magnificent animal chosen for the bullfighting ring. But Ferdinand prefers to smell the flowers instead of fighting and, eventually, after failing to engage the toreador, is returned to his pasture. According to the narration, he's sitting there still, under his cork tree, quietly smelling his flowers. He is happy. The flower-loving Resistance fighter may have been a thorn in the Germans' side, but unlike many of his companions, he refused to carry a gun. And — also unlike many of them — he survived to smell many more flowers, for, after his emigration to Canada, he was happy under his beloved Douglas firs in British Columbia, with perhaps one Disneyesque factor added: the botanist Vladimir Krajina suffered from hay fever.

⁂

In 1948 the Krajinas and my family took a winter vacation together in the Orlice Mountains. Shortly after New Year's Eve, Krajina, his daughter Milena, my father and I climbed on skis to the top of 1400-metre-high Kralický Sněžník. We had lunch there and then started to make our way down via another route.

Soon it began to snow and with the wind up it was obvious there was a blizzard in the making. In the middle of the woods we suddenly came upon a creek which had overflowed its banks and now had become a sheet of ice some five metres wide. What followed was proof of Krajina's uncanny ability to deal successfully with emergencies in his own ingenious way.

Because of the storm and approaching darkness we couldn't return to the hotel where we had eaten lunch. But going forward across the icy strip that extended down into the steep valley would be equally dangerous. While the rest of us stood about undecided, Krajina assessed the situation, then took command, ordering us to take off our coats and tie them together. Taking hold of one end, he lay down on the ice and, inch by inch, nudged himself to the other side, holding on to his metal-tipped ski pole with his other hand. With the aid of the combined coats onto which we held for dear life, his daughter Milena and I then followed his example, with Krajina on one side and my father on the other. The last one across was my father, following Krajina's example with the ski pole as a brake in case of a possible slip.

This quick-witted ability to solve difficult problems ranked right up there with Krajina's incredible survival instinct. Again and again it manifested itself with both Nazis and Communists.

Within months after the frozen stream episode came his and our escape to West Germany, following the February Communist takeover of Czechoslovakia. We were briefly interned with him in a Frankfurt refugee centre.

I did not see Krajina again until I arrived in Vancouver in the mid-1960s. By that time he was not only well established at the Botany Department of the University of British Columbia (UBC) but also as an important advisor to the provincial ministry of forests and of the forest industry.

The circumstances of his life may have changed but not his talents, boldness, determination or his loyalty to his friends and, in my case, loyalty even to their progeny. I was toying with the idea of graduate studies in the humanities during the 1960s, although my undergraduate grades were not that encouraging. The UBC department in question was not enthusiastic about admitting me, but Krajina knew very well that if a department member vouched for an applicant, the situation could change. Krajina approached a Czech student who had once spent a considerable amount of time at his house — now a junior member of the department in question — to ask him to present my case as my sponsor. The timid man begged off, explaining that it really wasn't the proper thing to do, presenting all sorts of excuses which Krajina found frivolous. It was obvious that the young professor was not about to risk his career just because it concerned a fellow Czech.

That, of course, was inimical to Krajina's conviction that when it concerned the fate of a countryman, a true patriot must be ready to put his hand into the fire. I recall him sadly informing me that nothing could be done, at the same time leaving no doubt as to what he now thought of his young protégé, whom until then he had considered a friend.

Fast forward about eight years: my first novel had been published in Toronto both in its original English and in a Czech translation. The reviews were exceptionally good, and I was resting on my laurels quite comfortably as a result.

A phone call from Vladimir Krajina came soon after. He had just finished reading my novel. Though now a patriotic Canadian, he still considered America to be the beacon of the free world and didn't like my frequent criticism of the U.S. in the novel. In his merciless opinion he noted that some of the chapters of the novel could have been easily published in the Czech Communist Party newspaper *Rudé Právo* — to help with its anti-American propaganda.

Thinking about it now, almost forty years later, I have come to the conclusion he may have been at least partially right. My intent had been to show how newly arrived, idealistic immigrants were sometimes unable to cope with America's idiosyncrasies, even blemishes. And for dramatic purposes I may have overstated them.

But here was Vladimir Krajina all over — unabashed, undeterred and unafraid of offending people when it came to stating what he believed to be the truth. Speaking to a first-time novelist in his thirties, the son of his good friend, he quite likely considered the call to be something of an educational nature. After all, he was a professor with impeccable credentials, even though these were hardly in literary criticism.

❦

Krajina straddled two different worlds during two different ages. More than half of his life would be spent in the new one, which provided him with great freedoms, while at times during his earlier life the restrictions placed on such freedoms were hardly imaginable.

He was born into a pre-World War I Central Europe in one of the most prosperous corners of the sprawling Austro-Hungarian Empire. It was a sleepy corner with its all-powerful emperor already seventy-five years old, an enviable age at the time. As a result, when steam engines were the norm and the first airplanes were taking to the air, his lands were run according to the horse-and-buggy customs of the early nineteenth century. Austria-Hungary was actually more comatose than sleepy. The first Czechoslovak president, Tomáš Garrigue Masaryk, estimated that his country would need fifty years for democracy to take a permanent hold. At the time of the Munich Agreement his country was barely twenty years old.

Despite his origins, Krajina adapted well to Canada. And many times. He may never have fully mastered the Queen's English (though some claim that he succeeded in transforming it into Krajina's Own), but he certainly understood the spirit of the land, its requirements and his duties. At the same time he contributed his bold forays in the quest of truth and his valiant attempts to do the right thing.

To some, Krajina's personage may seem an anachronism in this century imbued with post-modernist subjectivism and outright self-indulgence. But for most of us the idea that men of his moral fibre would be out of place at any period of human history is hard to fathom.

I

THE OLD
WORLD

1
Beginnings

VLADIMIR KRAJINA'S beginnings — had they been part of a Czech novel — probably would have been considered something of a cliché. Born in 1905 in a remote Moravian village into a large family with a wise father and caring mother, he was the youngest of six children. Only the oldest was another boy. The family circumstances were the staples not only of books but of Czech culture itself. Even the best-known Prague theatre personalities between the wars, Voskovec and Werich, had a hit song about a world traveller named Jack who was "originally from a Moravian hamlet."

In Vladimir's case his birth and early years took place in Slavice, a Moravian village so small it is not found on most Czech maps. His father was a progressive teacher who not only made sure that his students learned reading and arithmetic, but also practical skills and the newest farming methods. Hence Vladimir, before he was twelve, knew the names of common flowers and plants as well as how to prune fruit trees.

The school in Slavice where Krajina received his earliest education
from his father, who was the teacher.

When five, one year shy of school age, he took his savings and bought
his father a pouch of his favourite tobacco. After softening his father up
with the gift, he confessed he was somewhat bored and asked if he could
start school a year early. His amused father relented and for the rest of
his life Krajina never stopped learning. As if to add further to his general thirst for knowledge, the family lived in part of the school building
full of teaching aids.

Moravia and the other Czech lands further to the west were an important part of the Austro-Hungarian Empire. Although Czech was the
language of instruction in the lower grades (some believe that Moravians
speak better Czech than the Czechs themselves), German was taught in
secondary schools. It was certainly needed for any important career advancement.

But Slavice was not exactly remote. Brno, with its large German
minority, was not far away. So was Slavkov (Austerlitz in German). This

was where, in 1805, Napoleon had shown the Austrian Emperor who was boss. It is just a hop, skip and a holler from this Moravian capital.

The sleepy Slavice may have been thoroughly Czech, but Austrian influence was everywhere. Although his knowledge of German was far from perfect, the knowledge he had came in handy when in 1943, Krajina, as a Resistance prisoner, was confronted with the Nazi ruler of the Protectorate of Bohemia-Moravia, K.H. Frank. He then mustered his best German to explain what the Czechs thought of the Third Reich. And it was not a pretty picture.

Krajina's father was an all-around practical man, adept even at such things as making costumes for his daughters whenever there was a masquerade ball. He also played the organ in the local chapel. Krajina's happy childhood in Slavice came to an abrupt end when he was twelve. His father died suddenly and the family was forced to move to nearby Třebíč, which was already a town of considerable size. He began attending the *Gymnasium*, the academic secondary school there. It was there he met Marie and they became the Central European equivalent of high school sweethearts.

As a teenager, the world around Krajina changed once again, this time somewhat more thunderously. The Austro-Hungarian Empire, which had dominated the map of Europe for centuries, fell apart at the end of WWI, and the suffering of the war years was rewarded with the birth of the Czechoslovak Republic. It was the only state in the region which survived as a democracy until Hitler snuffed it out some twenty years later.

For those who have never experienced a democratic revolution, the enthusiasm of the times is hard to imagine. Krajina's willingness to risk his life over and over again in order to bring democracy about once more during World War II is almost certain to lie in this initial experience. In 1918 suddenly the whole world opened up. It no longer needed to be seen through Austrian eyes focused from Vienna, but through thoroughly Czech ones in Prague — the city where Krajina arrived during the early 1920s to begin his higher studies.

There the grandeur of the Bohemian Kingdom had been revived largely through the efforts of the republic's first president, Tomáš Garrigue Masaryk. Masaryk was a university professor who argued that the import of Czech history lay in the mediaeval Hussite times, when Czech kings were also Holy Roman Emperors, and also later, when Czech religious reformers shook Central Europe.

⁓

Krajina's interest in botany was fuelled by his brother Emanuel, who kept adding steadily to his already extensive herbarium. But there was also his interest in medicine, and he went to the university with the intention of becoming a doctor. The decisive fork in the road came shortly after Krajina started to study medicine — a fainting spell at the sight of his first cadaver, which made him switch to botany.

Charles University was founded in 1348, and Krajina enrolled at its Faculty of Natural Sciences 575 years later. He quickly became an outstanding student. In 1927 his research into the ecology of Slovakia's High Tatra Mountains was considered so important that he received his PhD at Charles University's Klementinum in a ceremony held exclusively for him. Krajina was also officially recognized by Tomáš Masaryk himself when he presented him with a personally inscribed gold watch.

During his time at the university, a fateful meeting occurred between Krajina and my father. It took place in Slovakia, at the so-called Votruba Hut, which was really a dormitory built by the Czechoslovak Army at the height of 1,675 metres following a territorial dispute with Poland. Father was on a hike through the Tatra Mountains with my grandfather when bad weather forced them to seek shelter in the hut. Not only was Krajina there with his students studying the alpine flora, but his sister was in charge of the housekeeping. Because of her excellent culinary skills, this refuge became more than adequate, and Krajina and Drábek struck up a friendship that lasted until their deaths in North America more than sixty years later. It was this friendship which eventually brought Krajina into the anti-Nazi underground.

In the 1920s, academic institutions abroad began taking notice of Krajina and, jointly with Bishop's Museum in Honolulu, Yale University awarded him a scholarship for the study of tropical flora in Hawaii. Much of the subsequent trip around the world in 1928 Krajina cap-

Krajina as a student at Charles University, Prague, with his
brother-in-law, the husband of Krajina's sister, Bohunka, 1926.

tured on a silent film. This film was thought to have been destroyed
forever when, during World War II, the Gestapo ransacked his empty
apartment in Prague's Pankrác quarter. Angry that Krajina had once
again eluded them, the Gestapo set all his belongings afire in the middle of the street. Another copy of the film was, however, found during
the 1990s. This was thanks to the vanity of Krajina's boss at the university, Professor Karel Domin (who later became the university's president for a short time). Wanting to be recognized, Domin had his name
appear in the film's titles in the same sized letters as Krajina's, and then
had a second copy made in the 1930s for the university's archives. It was
this copy which surfaced after the fall of the Iron Curtain.

Entitled *Aloha Oé* after a popular song of the time, the film begins by
detailing Krajina's five-day trip across the Atlantic aboard the USS
Leviathan. It then shows the Woolworth Building, New York's tallest
structure at the time, and follows him via the Caribbean, through the
Panama Canal to San Francisco, the region where Krajina encountered
giant sequoias for the first time. The Krajina-authored inter-titles describe them with appropriate awe.

And then the film explores Hawaii, "Four thousand kilometres from the U.S. shores and 6,400 from the Japanese ones," Krajina explains in one title. This comes just before informing us in a true professorial manner that hula can be danced either standing up or sitting down and is accompanied by the sound of "a rattling instrument." In the next frames Krajina explains that hula dancers' grass skirts are made from a plant of the *Cordyline terminalis* family and the headdress from *Plumeria acutifolia*. There follow shots of his climbs to the top of the volcanoes Waialeale on the island of Kauai and Kamakou at Molokai.

All in all, the film is impressive work. It indicates how Krajina had ensured that he was skilled in camera work, which he saw as an indispensable tool for a botanist. In total, it shows Japan, China, Singapore, India, Hawaii and Egypt, ending abruptly with the image of the Great Sphinx. Except for his fleeting shadow in one short take, there is not a single shot of Krajina himself in the entire film.

The film was made in 1928, when few people had heard of a phenomenon called Hitler. The Great Depression, which was to come a year later, was also something of an unimaginable development.

My father notes in his family memoir: "Then again I met Krajina in Prague. He was already serving as an assistant to Professor Domin, a well-known critic of President Beneš. Krajina did not share his political and other views, and his life was not made easy as a result. He lived very simply in some sort of a small kitchen behind the laboratory of the Botanical Institute in Benátská Street and that's where he brought one day his student love Marie whom he had just married."

And father continues: "Later, when we founded the club Přítomnost and entered politics, Krajina occasionally attended our meetings, but did not want to become active in any political party." That was likely because during those years Krajina was extremely busy as a vocal proponent of better working conditions for university lecturers, and he didn't want the struggle to be labelled political.

Vladimir Krajina's post-doctorial habilitation work in German, *Die Pflanzengesellschaften des Mlynica-Tales in den Vysoke Tatry* (The Plant Groups of the Mlynica Valley of the High Tatras), was published in 1934. One of his colleagues commented that "though a product of a single

Vladimir and Marie Krajina at their wedding in front
of the Prague City Hall, 1930.

scholar, this monograph excels in its (1) universal view of subalpine and
alpine plant life, (2) balanced evaluation of both phanerogamic and
cryptogramic plants, (3) year-round observations and measurements of
climatic and soil factors, and (4) integrated phytosociological synthe-
sis . . . of plant communities in the territory under study."

Even as early as 1934 Krajina was taking the integrated — in other
words the ecological — view of botany. He was now an associate professor (*mimořádný profesor*) of Geobotany and Plant Systematics at Charles
University in Prague.

In 1935 came the birth of his daughter Milena, who, although she loved her parents, later complained that relatively little time was devoted to her. No wonder. Krajina's wife Marie invariably accompanied him on study trips, while entrusting Milena to the care of her grandmother. These included France and England, where Krajina worked for London's Kew Gardens, specializing in tropical plants, and also Berlin. Some of these sojourns, such as the one in Berlin (despite the fact that Marie detested German cooking), were almost a year long.

Between the years 1929 and 1939 Krajina was publishing treatises, some of them definitive, on floral systems as diverse as those of the High Tatras and Hawaii. There was a lull in his botanical activity after 1939, but in 1942 — when he was already hiding from the Gestapo — his work on *Cibotium splendens* appeared, of all places, in Göteborg in neutral Sweden.

It was in Berlin that my father and Krajina met on foreign soil for the first time. My father, who was a Prague lawyer, was there on a business trip and recollected how the two of them saw a Nazi parade with goose-stepping SA members pass them on the street called Unter den Linden. Krajina's provocative statements and actions were so brazen that, as father notes in his memoirs, "to this day I wonder why the German police didn't arrest us on the spot. Though it took them a few more years, eventually they did catch up with us. But it was in Czechoslovakia."

2

The Birth of Resistance

THE CLOUDS GATHERING over Europe eventually resulted in a disaster called the Munich Agreement. In September 1938 Czechoslovakia lost 30 percent of its territory and a third of its population. The Germans then solemnly promised to leave the rump of the country alone. Hitler even went further, magnanimously stating he had no further territorial demands in all of Europe. The naïve French and English governments were convinced that they had successfully avoided a war.

No such conviction existed among most Czechs. Within weeks, President Beneš resigned and went into exile in London. Since, with one or two exceptions, the Czech government fell into the hands of decidedly weak individuals, it could do little. In fact, even this government was constantly being attacked by the rising wave of local Fascists. It was under these conditions that a group of determined professionals, soldiers and academics started meeting informally to plan clandestine resistance should the Germans invade. Vladimir Krajina, although at first he counted among the lesser-known members of the group, was one of them. Their priority was to maintain contact with the exiled president and inform him regularly about conditions at home.

My father became the initial courier, making two trips to London, supposedly to see his foreign clients. On his first trip he was even accompanied by my mother, and there was excitement from the start. Their train passed through Germany on November 9, the so-called Crystal Night, when the Nazis organized a pogrom which dwarfed all the previous pogroms. Several of its Jewish victims hid on the train, and a few even made it all the way to England, joyfully singing aboard the ferry from Ostende at the sight of the reassuring cliffs of Dover. Upon his return, father duly reported to his group what to expect under a Nazi rule.

During that visit, father promised President Beneš that they would maintain contact with London by all possible means. That promise was kept, mainly due to Krajina's efforts. In Prague the Resistance started calling itself the Political Centre and included members of all ideological views, with the exception of Fascists and Communists, the latter due to Stalin's ambiguous stance toward Nazism.

In January 1939, shortly after he returned from London for the second time, father was informed that his two "business trips" within weeks of one another (he had never been to London before) were becoming suspicious and the group decided Krajina should be asked to go next. Because of his comparative anonymity he was thought to be an ideal choice, and because of his previous stay in London and his background in botany, he could claim scientific research as his reason for going.

When asked, Krajina immediately agreed but also doubted that his head of department, Professor Domin, would let him go. He was right. Domin argued the department was too busy to spare Krajina for another of his trips abroad. It was also known that Domin, whose political orientation was extreme right, was certainly not a Beneš fan. Perhaps even more important was Domin's well-known vanity. He must have sensed Krajina's star was rising and wanted in no way to contribute to its glow. In the end Krajina didn't go because President Beneš had left London to lecture in the United States. Soon after, the Nazis occupied the rest of Czechoslovakia. It was clear that Britain would soon declare war and foreign travel for Czechs would be well nigh impossible.

Edvard Beneš.

⤫

At first glance it would seem that the Resistance movement was a direct conflict between the Nazi overlords and the Czech patriots, but this wasn't quite true. At least not initially. After the abdication of President Beneš in October 1938, and his subsequent departure into British exile, a new Czechoslovak president was elected, who was the former chief justice of the Supreme Court, Emil Hácha. The following March he was subjected to a highly humiliating experience by Adolf Hitler in Berlin. On the eve of the German occupation of his country, Hácha was given an injection and told to sign a document which stated: "The fate of the Czech nation I am placing with full trust into the hands of the Führer of the German nation."

When Hácha hesitated, Hermann Göring told him how sorry he would be if his air force was forced to destroy Prague due to his refusal. According to Göring this would have been necessary to prove to the still unbelieving British and French that the *Luftwaffe* was capable of doing its job perfectly.

After the occupation, Hácha remained the president of what was now the Nazi Protectorate of Bohemia and Moravia. His cabinet was headed by a prime minister who was a former Czech legionnaire and later general of the Czechoslovak Army, Alois Eliáš. The minister of agriculture was Ladislav Feierabend. While this government could not make the slightest move without the consent of the Nazi overlord, there were still small victories.

The first example of resistance came early in May 1939 when the government of the Czech Protectorate received an order from the office of the Nazi Protector to proclaim anti-Jewish laws, following the example of the notorious German Nuremberg Laws. There followed a long discussion whether cabinet should agree while at the same time try to win various exemptions for the Jews. One of the ministers claimed that no matter how much they were opposed, they would be unable to refuse the Nazis for long and suggested the Czech government should pass milder anti-Jewish laws. However, the majority of the ministers opposed giving in to the German demands.

Two weeks later another order came from the Protector's Office, this time in writing. The cabinet replied that since the Jews had been removed from important posts within the Protectorate it was unnecessary to pass special anti-Jewish laws.

Soon another written order arrived from the Germans, even more definite, and with a deadline attached. One of the ministers in the cabinet suggested informing the German Protector that the Czech government categorically rejected the idea of anti-Jewish laws, and he proposed that the government tender its resignation should the Germans insist on it. The proposal was accepted unanimously. Full of suspense, the Czech government awaited what would happen next.

Surprisingly, the Germans relented. They no longer pressed the Czech government but simply issued such laws as their own decrees. President Hácha played a large part in the government's resistance by fully supporting its decisions.

On the whole, this stand of the Czech government suited the Germans because it created at least a semblance of autonomy. The Protectorate president was even allowed to maintain a small and poorly armed army. (Because an order went out that each unit of this army must have its own band, the Czechs — with their proverbial humour — promptly renamed their government as Hácha's Melody Boys.)

The Czech government, which was supposedly acting as a buffer zone between the Nazi Protector and the population, also suited the Resistance, particularly since both Eliáš and Feierabend were active members of it. The various Czech ministries were useful tools in gathering information about such things as industrial and agricultural production as well as troop movements along Czech railways and highways.

At first Hácha was regularly briefed about Beneš' strategy in London. During this early phase of the Protectorate, Hácha still considered himself as an interim president who would eventually hand over the office to Beneš.

This soon changed. In January 1940, cabinet minister Feierabend's Resistance group was discovered by the Gestapo. Feierabend managed to escape only in the nick of time. His wife was arrested and spent several years in Ravensbrück concentration camp, together with Krajina's wife Marie. Later Feierabend became a member of the exile cabinet in London. In April of that year a memorandum was sent to His Majesty's Government asking for British recognition of this exile government. Beneš stated that the Czech Protectorate government with Hácha at its head "has already lost its influence and executive power. Today they are really only powerless puppets." The memorandum seemed to work. In September of that year Beneš was recognized by the British as the head of the legitimate government of Czechoslovakia.

Naturally, the Resistance at home had to take a stand on the position of the Protectorate government under Hácha, and this stance now became quite negative. In one message to London in April 1940, Krajina stated that from various news sources it was clear that the public is becoming critical of Hácha's actions, particularly when Hácha ended one of his telegrams to Hitler with the words *Sieg Heil.*

Hácha's position towards the Germans was, however, by no means clearly defined. At the end of 1940 a Resistance member sent, via Krajina's transmitter, the following message from Hácha to Beneš: "I am at your disposal whenever you wish it and I am looking forward to the day when I will hand over my office. You know to whom. But I will not enter Paradise with you. I will remain at the entrance."

That day Beneš' office chief wrote in his diary that the president had received news from home, noting that Beneš thinks Hácha will come out of his predicament with honour because he is aware of his role and he may even be able to save a few people from the hands of the Nazis.

At that time Krajina and other members of the Resistance must have realized that in some ways Hácha was certainly trying to help his own people. Again and again Hácha reminded the German Protector about the Czech prisoners in concentration camps, asking for their release, but was seldom listened to.

In the spring of 1941 Beneš was still at least nominally behind Hácha. He reminded the British that Hácha's signature on the occupation document two years before was the result of the Munich Agreement, not of his cowardice, thereby suggesting to the British that they must bear at least partial responsibility for his signature.

With the German invasion of Soviet Union in the summer of 1941, Hácha's role became even more difficult. Beneš' government advised him that, should the Germans demand an official public indictment of the exile government from the Protectorate government, he should resign.

The real crisis, however, came from another direction. Feierabend's escape, along with increased Resistance activity, convinced Berlin that a much stronger hand was needed in the Protectorate. With the arrival of Reinhard Heydrich in Prague as the deputy protector, martial law was declared and the reign of terror began. Before it was rescinded again, Prime Minister Eliáš was arrested and sentenced to death, although his execution did not take place immediately. By the end of January 1942, Nazi summary courts had sent almost five hundred people to their death and 2,242 to concentration camps.

After the assassination of Heydrich, martial law was declared once more, and Eliáš was executed along with scores of others. As far as Krajina and the Resistance were concerned, the Protectorate government, now composed solely of collaborators, was naturally devoid of all contact with the Resistance and, so far as the goal of liberation was concerned, thoroughly irrelevant.

Reinhard Heydrich (centre), Acting Reichsprotektor, in conversation with Horst Böhme (l) and Karl Hermann Frank (r), c. 1941.

Hácha's fate became increasingly sad. As a broken old man suffering from severe arteriosclerosis, he read the reports of thousands of his compatriots being sent to the Reich for slave labour, to concentration camps or to be executed. He tried to resign and even attempted to commit suicide, but was prevented from it by the ever-watchful Germans for whom his usefulness was not yet over. Eventually he withdrew to the presidential chateau at Lány. At the end of the war, when he was transported to the prison hospital at Prague's Pankrác, he was hardly conscious of where and who he was. He died of natural causes a few days later.

∽

When the Nazis occupied the rump of Czechoslovakia in March 1939, 173,000 people lost their jobs. These were employees of ministries that were abolished — such as Foreign Affairs and Defence. At first the German-controlled protectorate government tried to find employment for them in private businesses and in new institutions such as the supreme pricing office, but already early in 1940 Germany saw the burgeoning bureaucracy was really no solution. They next lowered the retirement age without fully realizing that they were thereby creating a new category of Czechs who were disgruntled and who now had ample time and reason to engage in the Resistance.

The largest group of those who had lost their jobs as a result of the occupation was the military. Some thirty thousand Czech officers and professional soldiers had been released from duty, and only a small part of them was recruited into the newly formed so-called Government Army of the Protectorate which was fully subordinated to the Germans.

The Nazis also proceeded to disband potentially dangerous organizations such as that of the World War I Legionnaires, who had served in foreign armies against the Central Powers. And when in the fall of 1939 the Germans closed the Czech universities, they produced another substantial group of both teachers and students, who now spent long hours in coffee houses. It was a demeaning existence devoid of substance, which tended to harden their conviction that they must somehow find a way to vent their anger at the occupiers. Nominally Krajina belonged to this category, although by the time of the Nazi occupation in March 1939 he had no time to sit in coffee houses: he was already heavily engaged in Resistance work.

Initially the Resistance groups were strongly influenced by the experience of the so-called Czech *Maffia*, which had resisted Austria-Hungary during the previous war. Several of its members had been sentenced to death for treason, although eventually they were pardoned and after the war played an important part in the new republic's political life. One member of the *Maffia* was the future president Beneš, who, during World War I managed to escape to France, and at the end of the war returned to the newly formed Czechoslovakia as minister of Foreign Affairs.

One early World War II Resistance group, headed by a well-known *Maffia* politician, used to meet in his elegant villa. Unfortunately, security there was minimal, with waiters serving meals and easily overhearing the group's most confidential plans. Inevitably, the group was soon discovered. One Gestapo member scathingly referred to it in garbled Czech as *kafíčko mafíčko* — something akin to a nice coffee klatsch mildly flavoured with conspiracy. Unfortunately, most of that group did not live to see the end of the war. As the Nazi's brutal suppression of any dissent within the Protectorate became evident, it was clear that the war conditions of WWI could no longer serve as a model. This is where Krajina, with his enormous self-discipline and strict observance of the rules of conspiracy, began to shine.

The beginnings of the Political Centre, the Resistance group to which Krajina initially belonged, were not without humour — a factor which totally evaporated with increased arrests, torture and executions. It was, for example, agreed that anybody arriving in London would introduce himself to Beneš with a postcard, showing the National Theatre in Prague. A man named Smutný (who would later became the president's chief of staff) was about to join Beneš in exile via neutral Turkey. The day before his departure he was visited by another member of the Resistance group who noticed the required card among Smutný's belongings. Turning it over he saw that Smutný had written "pass for B." on its reverse side — to remind himself of its function.

Krajina, who was increasingly involved in the work of the Political Centre, also had his problems with people who did not understand the need for secrecy. In the summer of 1939, a few months after the German occupation, two Czech priests, who were prominent in the Christian Democratic Party, decided to leave the country. Their lack of conspiratorial awareness showed even before their departure from Prague, when they threw a farewell party for themselves. It was Krajina who organized their escape to London via Poland, but when something didn't go as smoothly as they had expected, they didn't hesitate to call him long distance on a public phone from the Moravian border town, Bohunín. The pair eventually reached London safely, but several railway workers at Bohunín who had helped them ended up under arrest. Krajina himself this time somehow escaped the attention of the Gestapo.

An important escape for the Resistance in general, and Krajina in particular, was that of Colonel František Moravec on March 14, 1939. He had been alerted by a high-ranking German informant. One day before the German occupation of Prague, together with several fellow military espionage officers and a large load of intelligence material, he was flown out of Prague on a plane belonging to Dutch airlines. It would be this group with which Krajina's transmitters would eventually be in contact.

During the first few months of the German occupation, Krajina became one of the most energetic members of his Resistance group. It was primarily he who organized systematic monitoring of foreign broadcasts, and it was he who showed the greatest organizational genius by far. The purchase of powerful radio receivers was arranged. The multilingual students he recruited monitored the forbidden foreign broadcasts, then wrote nightly reports about what they heard. These reports were usually on the desks of the members of Resistance group the very next morning, so that they were adequately informed about the war and its needs so far as the Resistance movement was concerned.

The Political Centre was soon in close contact with its military equivalent, a group called the *Obrana národa* (Defence of the Nation), and yet another group consisting largely of union members, jointly organizing contact with the Allies via couriers and radio transmitters. These were manned by military personnel concentrated at the Prague city hall where they held cover jobs. Aside from those, there were many ancillary groups across the Protectorate, engaged in various activities such as arranging escapes, sabotage and strategic information gathering.

The radio operators were referred to as *musicians*. The coding and decoding duties were performed by civilians, in other words, *singers*, while the radio sets themselves became *threshers*. Through the exiled Josef Korbel (father of the woman who later became U.S. secretary of state, Madeleine Albright), a code was agreed upon based on identical dictionaries held in Prague and London. Experts considered it ingenious but it was never used — far more sophisticated systems replaced it. The complicated coding and decoding procedures were readily learned by Krajina and his wife, and the pair soon became accomplished *musicians*, a key cog in the operation of the transmitter.

Shortly before the war — about the middle of August 1939 — contact via the transmitter was established: first with Warsaw, later with Paris and eventually with London. Strangely enough, London — most likely because of the still strong influence of the Munich appeasers — initially didn't wish to be directly involved.

A problem arose when the Resistance movement became dominated by the Defence of the Nation, a group which consisted of former military personnel. Along with other groups, they initially considered the defeat of the Germans to be around the corner and saw the coming post-war period as crucial to the military for holding power while instituting reforms. Also for the adoption of a new constitution that would preclude the consequences of another Munich, namely surrender. Since Beneš would still be president of such a state, it wouldn't exactly be a military dictatorship. But since they saw a general in the second most powerful position, it would constitute something uncomfortably close to it.

With such an arrangement the ardent democrats in the Political Centre could never agree. On December 22, 1940, Krajina sent the following message to London: "The musicians [Defence of the Nation military group] are apparently preparing some sort of dictatorship of their own. . . . Now they are criticizing me because the transmitter is in my hands. They are supported by the labour union group. . . . It would be good if the musicians received instructions to pay greater attention to music [military affairs], rather than to the affairs of the singers [political ones]."

London replied that the fight against one dictatorship could not result in the establishment of another. On the other hand, London could see that the end of the war would come with military operations conducted on Czechoslovak territory. As a result, London indicated that during a short period without an effective government, the military might have to take over, but that this would in no way constitute a permanent military dictatorship. Eventually something of a compromise emerged, largely due to the general realization that the end of the war was not exactly around the corner and that the solution of other, more pressing problems would have to take precedence.

By April 1940, radio contact, which until then had been maintained only sporadically, was now taking place on a regular basis. It remained so until May of the following year, when one transmitter with three operators fell into the hands of the Gestapo. Within a month, however, contact with London was re-established and maintained until the beginning of October. While the technical side of the operation was handled by the military group, Krajina was in charge of the encoding and decoding of the messages, and thereby in practice controlled the content.

There were eleven transmitters and eight receivers in use, located in various places, all of them under Krajina's control. That year almost six thousand messages were sent out.

In addition to maintaining contact with the exiled President Beneš, the Political Centre organized an anti-German demonstration in Prague on October 28, 1939, the twenty-first anniversary of Czechoslovak independence. One of the demonstrators, a student named Jan Opletal, was killed by the Nazis. Further demonstrations took place at his funeral, with Krajina marching at the head of the funeral procession.

This time the repercussions were far more serious. The Germans ordered the closing of all Czech universities, executed nine student leaders and over a thousand students were sent to concentration camps. The Czech Botanical Institute, part of the Charles University of Prague, was also closed. Krajina was now without a job, but soon afterwards he was invited to visit the chairman of the German Botanical Institute in Prague and was offered a position there. Because the man began the interview by apologizing for the closing of the Czech schools, Krajina politely listened to his offer before rejecting it, explaining that he couldn't think of accepting such an offer without it being extended to all employees of his institute.

With the closing of the Czech Botanical Institute, a problem arose in finding a new place from which to transmit. It was initially solved by using various apartments of members of Krajina's group, and eventually by renting an apartment used exclusively for Resistance work.

Nevertheless, problems multiplied. A member of the Resistance was arrested shortly before Christmas. Improvidently he had kept notes about attendance at conspiratorial meetings, and these notes fell into the hands of the Gestapo. Several Resistance members were arrested and the transmissions were temporarily interrupted.

Because his name had been on the list, Krajina knew he was endangered. He had to make a crucial decision: should he attempt the difficult escape via Slovakia and Hungary to Yugoslavia and from there on to London, or should he go into hiding. Also endangered were the unofficial leader of the group, Prokop Drtina, and my father. As a former assistant to President Beneš and unsure of how he would cope if tortured,

Drtina feared the Gestapo could force him to make statements against the exiled president. He chose to flee, while father and Krajina decided to stay.

Krajina now devoted all his time to Resistance work. He decoded messages received from London, met with other Resistance members and gathered information about the situation throughout the country, which had been renamed the Protectorate of Bohemia Moravia.

Although he was seldom at home and often stayed with friends, it wasn't until the following spring, in 1941, that he cut his ties with his family entirely. There had been a wave of arrests, and it was now certain the Germans were on his trail. Krajina and Marie decided that one of them should stay with their six-year-old daughter. He left his wedding ring with his mother-in-law, along with a letter to Marie to be shown to the Gestapo. It informed her that he was leaving her for another woman. Krajina commented many years later: "It was a difficult decision for both of us. My wife bravely bore this, which made a tremendous impression on me. Even though we were apart so much, during the war we had grown together into one solid trunk of a tree against which all storms were ineffective."

The long months in hiding would have broken an ordinary man, but Krajina was far from an ordinary man. Working night and day, and hiding at various places in Prague while his co-conspirators were being hunted down and arrested one by one, he kept up radio contact with London with only short interruptions until the middle of 1942. Even after that he managed to send out messages sporadically. By the time he was arrested the following year, around twenty thousand of them had been sent and some six thousand received.

My father's reminiscences of those times included this passage: "The Gestapo left me at large, as we quickly realized, only to get on Krajina's trail through me. At that time he was already in hiding. As a result, our fates between 1940 and 1942 were closely tied together even though we could meet only rarely and at night.

"From these difficult times I have one very dear and for him a rather typical memory. I think it was before Christmas 1941 when Krajina was hiding somewhere in the Spořilov section of Prague, although I was never supposed to know for security reasons exactly where. We met on that frosty morning on the dark streets somewhere in Michle. His situation at that time was terribly sad. He slept covered by featherbeds on an open veranda, without knowing what was happening to his wife Marie, what was the situation at home and whether he himself would be able to stay in hiding.

"I felt sorry for him because I was somewhat better off. I could be with my family and there were even times when I started to believe that the Gestapo had forgotten all about me. One night I brought with me a present for Krajina — a beautiful edition of Josef Mánes' drawings, entitled *Czech Flowers*. Krajina was delighted to have it. But when, after the assassination of Heydrich, more difficult times arrived, Krajina sent the book back to me to hide it. I opened it and discovered that despite all the suffering and danger, he was not able to suppress the botanist in him. On various pages there were notes written in pencil as he corrected the inaccurate or wrong names for the flowers by Master Mánes."

Despite his personal misery, the most valuable messages were sent to London by Krajina's team during this time, based on information provided by Paul Thümmel, a highly-placed member of the German *Abwehr* (Counter-intelligence) staff. The Resistance had recruited Thümmel even before the war, and he was now conveniently stationed in Prague. Executed towards the end of the war, Thümmel never fully explained why he cooperated with the Czechs. Observing the conspirator's rule that the fewer people an underground worker knew the fewer he could betray under torture, Krajina never met Thümmel or knew his name. Through military Resistance group members, he knew only that the source was trustworthy and the information extremely valuable.

With their ranks greatly thinned out by arrests, it was thought wise for the three leading Prague-based Resistance organizations to consolidate. With further losses, Krajina eventually became the acknowledged leader of a new group, called *ÚVOD*. The word in Czech means "introduction," but it was also an acronym for an organization called the Central Council of Home Resistance.

With each arrest of a Resistance member, there was the danger of his betraying the cover names of others, so these had to be changed immediately. On average, each member of Krajina's group had at least two names, but Krajina topped them all with eleven. It reflects not only his importance but also one of the reasons he remained out of the grasp of the Gestapo for so long.

Early in December 1941, Krajina's team sent a radio message to London with information acquired from Thümmel about a confidential speech given by Marshal Keitel. It indicated that the Germans would delay their attack on the USSR until England was subdued. "In the spring of 1941 England, as an island, will be ripe for our invasion," Keitel said, and Krajina immediately considered it his duty to make sure that Stalin did not wait until Britain was on its knees.

Here Thümmel helped once again, providing Krajina's group with a list of Nazi agents active in the USSR. The list was promptly handed over to the Soviet consul in Prague, but there was no apparent reaction, let alone expression of gratitude from the Soviets.

Late that same year, Krajina's group sent one of its most valuable messages acquired from Thümmel: the Germans were moving their *Wehrmacht* units from the shores of the Atlantic to the Mediterranean, obviously planning an invasion of Crete, Cypress and eventually Syria in order to threaten British-controlled Egypt and the Suez Canal. Because of this message, the British received a warning some two months in advance, and Churchill was able to take effective precautions. In his reminiscences Krajina labelled it as "an outstanding success of our intelligence service."

There followed others. Krajina's group warned Stalin twice that a German invasion of the Soviet Union was imminent. The first message went out in April 1941. It stated that Hitler had decided against further dialogue and would attack the Soviets on April 18. According to Thümmel, the date was revealed to the Führer by the formation of flying birds, an old Roman mystical sign which Hitler believed. The *Luftwaffe* would first bomb Soviet aircraft on the ground along the attack line for two hours. Krajina's message advised Stalin to move his air force further inland.

Nothing like that happened. Stalin was highly suspicious of information coming from non-Communist sources, sometimes even from Communist ones. Hitler's invasion date was eventually postponed because of his need to neutralize the Balkans first, and this could have added to Stalin's suspicions.

Stalin was warned once more via Krajina's transmitter in June 1941. This time Krajina couldn't resist including a suggestion for the British to provide help only on condition that Stalin democratize his domain. After the war Churchill explained to Krajina why this was not acted upon: Britain needed Russia as an ally under *any* conditions.

Stalin didn't heed even this second warning. As a result, on June 22, the *Luftwaffe* destroyed a substantial part of the Soviet air force while still on the ground. Thousands of lives were needlessly lost as well.

There were other important messages sent to London. Some dealt with the production of new armoured cars at the Škoda works, the movements of Nazi units and even weather conditions over the Protectorate, which were important for the Allies' air operations.

There were also protest actions on the ground within the Protectorate, which were organized with the help of London's short-wave Czech broadcasts. In September, a boycott of the Nazi-controlled Protectorate newspapers was organized by Krajina's group. It turned out to be an enormous success. Even the street vendors — who stood to lose the most by the action — pleaded with their customers not to buy their wares.

Shortly before the German invasion of Russia, Krajina's wife Marie received a summons to report to the Gestapo. When she arrived, she tried to defend herself with Krajina's letter about his unfaithfulness, but to no avail. After a few days in a Prague prison she was sent to the Ravensbrück concentration camp.

The Resistance messenger whose duty it was to let Krajina know about the arrest later noted that for some time he concentrated on other news because he couldn't find enough courage to tell him. When he finally did tell him, he reported that Krajina was initially shocked by the news but quickly recovered. His face tightened with resolve, and he said through his clenched teeth: "If they think they'll get me this way, they are wrong. Absolutely wrong!"

3

The Noose Tightens

REINHARD HEYDRICH, the second-highest-ranking SS officer in the German Reich, had been appointed Acting *Reichsprotektor* of the Protectorate of Bohemia Moravia in September 1941. The day after his arrival in Prague he declared martial law and, by the time it was lifted two months later, over four hundred people had been executed, including the mayor of Prague and the prime minister of the Protectorate cabinet.

In a secret speech delivered to his confidantes not too long after he assumed his post, Heydrich described the nature and extent of the Czech Resistance as follows:

> It was far more extensive and dangerous than we expected. If we now, after four months, judge our performance against the Czech intelligence service on a purely technical basis, we note that in that time we have secured some 90 short-wave transmitters. We also note that the number of martial law judgements is somewhere between 400 and 500, that the number of arrests was between four and five thousand.

These numbers make it clear — and this is important to stress — that as characterized by those people who have been arrested and sentenced to death, we are dealing with an organization of generally high spiritual values. These were not people who had simply been carried along by the stream; they constitute the leading machinery! From the preceding you can see what would have happened had we not taken emphatic steps on principle. . . . We have managed to destroy the Resistance movement before it was able to influence the wider masses in any significant measure.

But he was mistaken. Resistance activity had been merely disrupted by his martial law, certainly not destroyed. In fact, when Krajina and his group began to suspect that London planned to assassinate Heydrich, possibly as a response to his martial law and harsh measures, they strongly opposed the action. In their messages they warned that German reprisals would so totally disrupt the information-gathering function of the Resistance that it would not be able to recover from it.

The Czech Resistance knew that when it came to intelligence gathering they were in first place among all occupied countries. Consequently they couldn't understand why they should be required to prove their existence by some admittedly dramatic but in the long run extremely costly act. Earlier, President Beneš had sent the following message to the Czech Resistance: "Your work is bringing for us here political successes. The British value your work that much more since they constantly compare them with the results of the Poles, the Dutch and others who are unable to come up with anything like it. Not even the French can match it. Your work therefore actively helps the good name of our entire nation."

And an entirely different source was praising the Czech Resistance as well when the military propaganda section of the Office of the *Reichsprotektor* reported: "The Czech broadcasts from London over the BBC show excellent knowledge even of internal happenings in the Protectorate. They take an immediate stand even on the least significant events."

In his book *Czechs under the German Protectorate*, Detlef Brandes claims that in 1940 almost six thousand messages were sent to London. In December of that year alone there had been 1,283 of them and their number was constantly rising. "All the transmitters and all their operators were under Krajina's control," writes Brandes, and then goes on to explain that the messages could be divided into political, military and economic categories. The military sort reached a particularly high level of accuracy. These included information about German war plans and the dispersal of *Wehrmacht* units, also reports about war material production and transports across the Protectorate. They were supplied by railway workers, postal employees and illegal cells in war plants.

To the very last moment the home Resistance remained hopeful that President Beneš as well as Winston Churchill would understand that to go ahead with Heydrich's assassination would mean a serious disruption of their work. Unfortunately they didn't. Early in 1942 Czech and Slovak commando-parachutists were dropped from a British plane with a mission to assassinate "Hangman" Heydrich. They even met with Krajina. The nature of their mission was strongly suspected by the Resistance from the moment of their arrival, but the parachutists steadfastly refused to acknowledge this was their assignment.

"I tried to explain to them why ÚVOD is opposed to the idea of assassination but was not successful," Krajina later noted. "The parachutists must have been convinced that they were bound by their orders and their pledge for their mission. They had volunteered for it, never allowing for the possibility that here at home someone could attempt to talk them out of it, that the home-based Resistance could have an opinion about this. I respected it; if this was an order of the exile government which was now internationally recognized it had to be carried out. . . . On that spring Saturday evening we walked along the darkened streets of Prague. Calmly I tried to talk the trio out of their assignment which they denied they had. . . . Only after the war did I find out that they had given their pledge [to assassinate Heydrich] to President Beneš personally."

In an attempt to find out how the parachutists would respond, Krajina even casually mentioned to them that the castle at Panenské Břežany was Heydrich's residence, suggesting that they may want to know more about the place. But even then the parachutists didn't betray their mission. When he was shaking their hand and saying goodbye to them, Krajina had a premonition that he was doing it for the last time. He studied their faces, noting that they had the look of outstanding men. Their exemplary military training was clearly obvious in their personalities.

Krajina returned to his hideout at the Drašner family apartment with mixed emotions. On the one hand he was impressed by the strength and determination of the exile government; on the other he regretted what he felt was insufficient concern for the needs of the Resistance at home.

The Drašners and their young son were a deeply religious family who belonged to the Protestant Czech Brethren. They considered it their moral duty to resist Hitler. It was at their house Krajina had the first of his three harrowing experiences. In October 1941 the Gestapo unexpectedly arrived to search the premises. At the last moment Krajina simply hid behind a clothes closet, helped by the fact that such closets in Europe were not built into the wall. The lazy Gestapo man opened the door and looked around without actually entering the room, and Krajina was saved.

If the Gestapo had searched the apartment, Krajina would have been discovered and almost certainly shot shortly thereafter. It was before the decisive German defeat at Stalingrad, and their arrogance knew no bounds.

Shaken by the experience, the very next morning Krajina sought refuge with a Prague family, the Rozums. When he rang their apartment bell, however, the ashen-faced Mrs. Rozum told him to run as fast as he could, and to keep running. Ten minutes earlier both her husband and her son had been arrested by the Gestapo. Stunned by the news, Krajina staggered back on the street.

Later that year, just before Christmas, he was hiding in Prague with the Patzel family when the Germans came to the door once more, looking for their son Marian. Mrs. Patzel lied convincingly, telling them that he worked at the Škoda Works in Mladá Boleslav, when in reality he was serving in Tobruk with the Czech contingent of the British Army. She even admonished them, ever so gently, for not looking for Marian at Mladá Boleslav. The confused Gestapo left, and Krajina, who was watching the scene with bated breath from behind a wooden railing on the floor above, was saved again.

Despite these narrow escapes and despite the fact that Krajina's group had lost their transmitter after a successful Gestapo raid on another apartment, they continued sending messages to London with a new transmitter provided by another group of parachutists.

⁓

The most spectacular and costly act of Czech resistance against the Nazis was the assassination of *Reichsprotektor* of Bohemia-Moravia, Reinhard Heydrich on May 27, 1942. During the ambush, a Sten gun jammed at a crucial moment, and another parachutist threw a bomb at his car. Heydrich, who was riding to Prague from his chateau in the outskirts of the city in an open Mercedes, was badly wounded and died eight days later.

The background of the assassination remains murky to this day. While there were reports that President Beneš had met with the parachutists just before their departure, he told others that he knew nothing about Heydrich's assassination, that it had been planned by the chief of intelligence, Moravec, together with the British.

Reinhard Heydrich's car after the attack on May 27, 1942, by
Czech and Slovak soldiers who were parachuted in from England.

On the day of Heydrich's assassination, Krajina was back at the Drašners. The Gestapo arrived there that evening once more, this time searching for the assassins. Totally surprised by their arrival, Krajina managed at the last moment to suspend himself in a light shaft. He wrote later how "with my left hand I held on to a relatively strong curtain cord, while with my right one I held on to the windowsill. During those interminable twenty minutes I grew stiff with tension."

In the middle of June, Heydrich's assassins were cornered in a Prague church along with other parachutists. They put up a valiant fight for several hours. Some were killed, others committed suicide when they saw all was lost. In the end, none of the parachutists in the church survived.

Krajina then decided to leave Prague. It was late spring 1942 and the botanist Krajina, the classic product of the countryside, wasn't sorry to be leaving the sad shell of a once thriving city. He decided to head to Turnov, a town some eighty kilometres to the north, in the middle of one of the most scenic regions of the country called the Czech Paradise.

ᘒᘒ

What kind of a city was it that Krajina was leaving after more than two years of German occupation? Certainly not a happy one. Formerly known as one of the sparkling capitals of Europe, Prague was now shrouded in the darkness of a wartime blackout with its men and women forced to put in ten-hour days on behalf of the Nazi war effort. Everything had been progressively geared to the Reich's needs. In a few days after the start of the occupation, all signage, including storefronts, had to be bilingual with German always placed above Czech. The notorious Jewish transports to Terezín (Theresienstadt in German) began soon after, and from there prisoners were sent to the death camps. Each week frightened people could be seen assembling for the transports near the Prague fairgrounds.

The newspapers and all other media were in the hands of collaborators. A good example is the following commentary from a newspaper called *Polední list* (*The Noon Newspaper*) praising the establishment of the notorious Warsaw Ghetto: "The Warsaw example shows clearly how to solve the Jewish problem. . . . All that what happened here so far, forbidding them to sit in cafes, ride in the first cars of the trams, visit movie houses and theatres, shop only during certain hours, are only inadequate half-measures. The Jews are getting around such regulations, they indulge in the black market, in whispered propaganda and they provoke the Czech people. They still constitute the destructive element which permeates the Czech population, bothers it by defeatist propaganda, secretly continuing to exploit it by profiteering in the black market."

The black market certainly flourished but it had little to do with the Jews. Although the imposed favourable exchange rate for the German currency enabled the first German soldiers arriving in Prague in March 1939 to gorge themselves on cheaply acquired delicacies, delicacies which had long ago disappeared from the Reich's shops, within months there were food shortages, and rationing was put in place in the Protectorate. Prices began to rise astronomically: the highest-paid Czech worker received less than 3,000 crowns a month while a pair of shoes cost 3,500 crowns and a suit 15,000. Although those active in the black market were severely punished by the Germans, the market itself flourished. With fuel shortages becoming ever more dire, apartments were seldom heated, and the city was frequently plagued by power shortages.

Between May 28 and September 1, 1942, over three thousand Czechs were arrested. Exactly 1,357 of them were executed for various reasons, such as illegal arms possession, or failure to register with the police. The largest numbers of those shot were found guilty of "agreeing with the assassination."

Notorious pinkish-red notices on street corners carried lists of those who had been executed by the Gestapo the previous week, while fearsome accounts of the Gestapo's cruelties circulated through the city. In addition, by the end of 1942, almost eighty thousand young Czechs had been sent to the German Reich for slave labour.

∽

Having successfully passed a train inspection of his false documents identifying him as Jan Dočekal, Krajina was welcomed in Turnov by a minister of the Protestant Czech Brethren. The same night he was taken to a secluded cottage near the woods and, with its owner, visited a nearby cave used by the local Resistance group as a warehouse. Krajina made a mental note that in an emergency it could be used as a hiding place.

Even that stay was short because Turnov, with its sizeable Gestapo contingent, was much too near. The very next day Krajina started for another hiding place with his coding material. He kept a leisurely pace, occasionally stopping to smell the wild plants. "All day I smelled thyme which grew on the surrounding hills in great abundance," he noted. Reaching his destination at Drahoňovice towards the evening, he was convinced this was where he would finally be able to relax. At least for a while.

Instead, it was at Drahoňovice that he found by listening to the radio announcements that his brother Emanuel was among those shot as part of the mass executions following Heydrich's assassination. Krajina's daughter, Milena, says that until the end of his life her father couldn't rid himself of a guilty feeling that somehow his Resistance activity caused his brother's death. There is no proof of that: the Gestapo simply selected their victims at random from those walking in the city square. It is highly unlikely that they put his name together with the man being hunted in the Czech Paradise.

The day after his arrival in Drahoňovice, Krajina was accompanied by friends to a more secluded location near a place called Děčín, where a family, the Koldas, lived. But the hoped-for safe refuge was not to be. One of his co-conspirators, who had visited Krajina when he was still at Drahoňovice, was captured after a shootout near Pilsen. Badly wounded, he was subjected to unbearable torture during which the Gestapo poured salt and pepper into his stomach wound. In agonizing pain he eventually divulged Krajina's hiding place, hoping that Krajina would have time to escape.

Krajina, of course, was no longer at Drahoňovice, but the Gestapo now systematically began to comb the entire region. From his gabled window at the Kolda house, Krajina one day noticed a couple of suspicious characters. Although they were dressed like tourists, from his hideout he could hear their German-accented Czech. Later he saw them again watching the house through binoculars. He wasn't sure if they had recognized him because the picture which authorities had been given showed him without a beard, but he took no chances and moved into the cave which he had discovered the first day in the region.

In the meantime Krajina's former hosts, the Koldas, were visited by the Gestapo, who wanted to know who lived with them. They denied that anyone did except, of course, for an occasional visit of Kolda's sister. Then to ease whatever suspicion that may have been left, they good-naturedly offered to put up the two Gestapo men while they were supposedly on holidays. For two weeks, Mrs. Kolda cooked delicious meals, while Mr. Kolda informed everyone around who the men were and warned them to watch what they said.

Krajina soon moved to yet another hideout in a place called Kacanovy. Posing as a tourist in a well-known tourist region, he even ventured to the local pub, and sat with the locals underneath a linden tree, wearing his hat with a jackdaw feather on its side. He drank beer and, as he wrote later, "talked philosophy" with them. At the same time he tried his best, at least temporarily, to cut off all contacts with his colleagues in the Resistance.

But to no avail. Against his wishes he was visited by some of them who were later arrested. It would be only matter of time before the Gestapo arrived at his hideout.

That time came sooner than expected — on Thursday, August 20. Before dawn the Gestapo surrounded the village. The dogs began to bark and the servant woman came running into Krajina's room to tell him that the Gestapo was in the village. Krajina's first thought was to take the cyanide he carried in his pocket. But the owner of the villa then entered and urged Krajina to try to get away at all costs, helping him to put his pants on over his pajamas. Stuffing coding material and his two fake identification cards into a bag, and still in his slippers, Krajina ran quickly down the back stairs to the garden. He jumped over a fence and began zigzagging through a potato field while dodging bullets.

Hans Otto Gall, who later began working with the Resistance, was a member the Gestapo team there that morning. Gall, an expert shot, used to tell how he fired repeatedly at the zigzagging figure but missed every time. "It seemed like the man wasn't human," he would recall.

Several things helped Krajina to escape. There was much confusion surrounding the scene — the raid hadn't been properly organized. Then the caretaker Studnička who, like Krajina, had a gold crown on his front teeth, was mistaken for the Resistance hero, and shot and killed by the Gestapo. More confusion ensued.

Just how close Krajina came to being shot was indicated by the bullet hole he later found in his hat with the jackdaw feather on its side. All that day he kept running, avoiding people and crossroads, although eventually he did stop at a farmhouse, where he asked an old friend for shoes and bread, which he was promptly given.

Krajina's subsequent frantic journey through the countryside while pursued by the Gestapo became the subject for a work by a Czech poet who was vacationing there, unaware of who it was the Gestapo was after. His work became a popular epic poem called "The Ballad of the Czech Paradise."

Deathly tired, Krajina was put up in the attic of a local businessman at a town called Železný Brod, immediately falling asleep in a stack of freshly cut hay. At midnight he woke up with an excruciating headache. He was also violently ill and immediately understood that his hay fever had returned with a vengeance. He headed out to walk it off on the street, a procedure he was forced to repeat each night that he spent there.

After a few days Krajina found refuge with a man called Hlaváček, a patriotic principal of a school at the village Veselá. The hiding place, especially built for him and two other fugitives behind a false wall, seemed ideal.

4

The Arrest

ON THURSDAY OCTOBER 24, 1942, without Krajina knowing it, his situation became substantially more complicated. That day another group of three Czech paratroopers, designated in Britain as "Antimony," was dropped some forty kilometres from where Krajina was hiding.

He had been silent for quite some time, and London was worried, suspecting that either he or his transmitter had been captured. As an extra precaution, the Antimony team now carried three new machines. Twice in the past the British had been told that the Gestapo had caught Krajina, but the information had proven false and each time he was heard from again. The Antimony team carried with them a letter for Krajina or his successor from President Beneš.

The message also dealt with Heydrich's assassination. In it Beneš wrote: "All the persecution had, in one sense, helped us. It was terrible but it returned us to an honourable place in the world and placed us among the fighting nations." Krajina was less enthusiastic about the "help" Beneš wrote about. On the day that Antimony landed, 350 Czech men and women were executed at the Mauthausen concentration camp. Their only crime was that their names were either Kubiš or Valčík — the same as two of the assassins.

Also on that day in the same concentration camp three members of the Drašner family who had hidden Krajina in Prague were executed, although not because of Krajina. Four others who were executed, however, *had* helped to hide Krajina in the Czech Paradise region.

Despite their rigorous training, the parachutists had little idea just how dire the situation in the Protectorate had become since the Heydrich assassination. In England they had been provided with the cover names for people in the Resistance and had been told it would be useful if they managed to make contact with them. One belonged to Captain Morávek from the military Resistance group (who, however, had by then already been killed in a shootout with the Gestapo). Another was a man named Jindra, one of the cover names for the super agent Thümmel, but he too had already been uncovered by the Germans. A third person was someone with a curious name. The Antimony team was told: "It could happen that you will make contact with the name Buk or Dub. That would be excellent. Under this name hides our most effective and crafty revolutionary worker."

Dub and Buk were Krajina's cover names. Late in November, Hlaváček, in whose house Krajina was hiding, managed to arrange a meeting between Krajina and the Antimony team. They brought one transmitter with them, the other two having been taken over by a Communist underground group trying to establish contact with Moscow.

Despite enormous difficulties, at the end of 1942 Krajina and his friends managed to renew radio contact with London. On January 3, a reply came from Beneš. It surmised correctly that with the Soviet victory at Stalingrad a great danger for Russia had been averted, but it also, quite incorrectly, predicted that a western front would soon be opened on the European continent. This last prediction was off by more than a year.

January 1943 was the last month of Krajina's freedom. After his hiding place behind a false wall had miraculously remained undiscovered when the Gestapo came to arrest Hlaváček, Krajina realized he could no longer stay there. Once more he was on the run, managing to get word to the Antimony parachutists hiding nearby that with Hlaváček's arrest they too were in grave danger.

While being taken away by the Gestapo, Hlaváček tried to cut his wrists, but the bleeding was discovered and his life was saved. At the Gestapo headquarters he was confronted with a colleague on his last legs who pleaded with him to tell the Germans the whereabouts of the parachutists — to end all his terrible suffering. Hlaváček steadfastly refused. Then the Gestapo used what turned out to be their trump card: they threatened to level Hlaváček's village to the ground, killing all the inhabitants — as they had done at Lidice after Heydrich's assassination. The shaken Hlaváček asked for a moment to think it over. Quite likely this devout Czech Protestant used the time for a prayer, asking for divine guidance.

After a few minutes alone, he agreed to help with the capture of the parachutists, but only on condition that neither they nor those connected with them would be harmed. Surprisingly, the Gestapo acquiesced, even insisting that the whole agreement be put on paper.

While interrogating Hlaváček and others, the Gestapo men came to realize that the Antimony parachutists did not come — as they had thought — to assassinate K.H. Frank, now the highest Nazi police official in the Protectorate. Their mission had been rather to re-establish radio contact between the Czech Resistance and London. The Gestapo eventually found the hiding place which Krajina had been forced to leave so quickly. Inside were found charred encoded messages and coding material.

The Gestapo now knew they had a chance to catch both Krajina and the Antimony team. Hlaváček was brought before K.H. Frank in Prague, and the agreement was officially extended to Krajina and his colleagues — but only if Krajina could be caught within four days. They released Hlaváček and, suprisingly, did not have him followed. The Germans also hurriedly brought Krajina's wife Marie from Ravensbrück to be used as bait.

Not long after, the Gestapo discovered the hiding place of the Antimony team of parachutists at Rovensko. Anxious to capture them alive, the Germans surrounded the house, making the Czech police go in first. The policemen informed the parachutists about the arrangement, and they agreed to be taken by the Czech policemen. In the bright spotlight one of the policemen led them toward a Gestapo man named Leimer, who would later play an important role in dealing with Krajina. Leimer heard one parachutist crunch something between his teeth, and a few moments later saw him collapse. Then he saw his comrade collapse beside him.

"You'll never get us alive," Jasínek, the third parachutist, calmly told the Gestapo.

The frantic Germans loaded the poisoned Antimony team into a car and raced towards the nearest doctor's office. There, to Leimer's protests, a brave Czech policeman lit Jasínek's last cigarette. Then Jasínek too felt the effect of the poison he had swallowed and fell into the arms of the same Czech policeman. Soon afterwards all three parachutists were pronounced dead. The work of the Antimony team was over.

Hlaváček was still at large, however, thanks to his agreement with

Identity card of SS Officer Willi Leimer, who arrested Krajina in 1943 and then surrendered to him in 1945 at the end of the war.

the Gestapo. He found Krajina and pleaded with him to give himself up. Krajina refused, explaining that as an underground leader he could not do so. He said he was bound by his duty as a Czech patriot, adding that he did not consider this duty to be a hindrance but a great honour. Should he fall into the hands of the Gestapo, it would be as a dead or dying man after the example of the parachutists. If he gave up while still alive he would surely be judged harshly by his nation after the war.

Krajina also told Hlaváček that he could not honour any agreement with the Germans who had killed his brother. He advised Hlaváček that if he wished to rejoin the Resistance and go into hiding, he would be welcomed. Hlaváček sadly shook his head.

When the two men embraced and said goodbye, Krajina felt that neither of them was happy with the results of their negotiations. He could see that he had not managed to shake Hlaváček's faith in the agreement with the Gestapo. Krajina told him to report to the Germans that he had not found him.

With the parachutists dead and the Gestapo combing the area, it was only a matter of time before Krajina would be captured. At the time, Krajina was hiding with a family which had been found by the merchant Drbohlav. After leaving Krajina in his new hiding place, Drbohlav went home, where he was surprised by the Gestapo. Again torture followed, including electric shocks. Krajina's colleagues were being arrested one by one. The wily Gestapo was alternately applying pressure via threats and torture, then reminding everyone of the Hlaváček agreement and reporting that even Krajina's wife Marie favoured his surrender to prevent further bloodshed. They sensed they were getting closer.

The end of the chase came on the night of January 31, 1943. Krajina himself described it this way: "After listening to the regular London broadcast I was getting ready to go to sleep. Suddenly, out of nowhere, with my hosts being caught unawares, the nearby streets were full of German uniforms. Their reflectors were providing light as if it was the middle of the day. . . . I reached into my vest for a glass vial which I carried with me constantly since 1939, but without paying attention to the fact that the powder in it was no longer white but yellow. I prepared to enter eternity. . . . In the next moment they were inside, running up the steps. While screaming Open! Gestapo! they banged at the door. . . . Eventually they broke it down and the Gestapo men Leimer and Nacht-man recognized me right away from my photograph. Nachtman reached into my mouth with his boxer's hand, while I managed to swallow the rest of the poison. I was convinced I had enough arsenic in me to kill several people, certain they would not get me alive. But the Gestapo was ready. They brought milk with them, which they poured into me. Nacht-man had cut his hand on the vial in my mouth and was now more wor-ried about his own life than mine. Blood was coming out of my mouth. Leimer had brought a stomach pump and, using force, applied it to me."

The arsenic that Krajina had carried in the pocket of his vest for four years was less effective because of its interaction with carbon dioxide, which had created an acidic reaction. The carbon dioxide now coated every grain of the arsenic. That and the quick action of the Gestapo saved Krajina's life, although even the arsenic's weakened state had some frightening effects.

"I saw everything in yellow and as a photographic negative. The light places were dark and dark ones seemed lighter. The Gestapo men carried me down into the car with Leimer's voice ordering: *Halt! Bitte nach Krankenhaus!* (Halt! To the hospital please!). At the hospital in Turnov my stomach was pumped out several times more. My vision was returning to normal. At times I reproved myself for not carrying a revolver, but in the next moment I realized it would have meant certa-in death for my friends, without any trial. Poison in possession of those being arrested was tolerated but a weapon was not. Our death did not bother the Gestapo nearly as much as the mere possibility of their own."

The next twenty-seven months of Krajina's life would be spent in Nazi captivity.

5

In Captivity I

KRAJINA CERTAINLY wasn't feeling at all well in the Gestapo car on the way to Prague. His larynx had been scraped and his stomach bruised. But worst of all, he was still alive. Not knowing that the weakened arsenic was the reason he wasn't yet facing eternity, he was regretting that he did not resist the stomach-cleansing procedure more vigorously.

He was riding in the same car with his arresting Gestapo men, Nachtman and Leimer, who never stopped consoling him that everything would be all right now and that he would soon see his wife. And sure enough, on the way to Prague they picked up Marie, whom he hadn't seen for more than two years, and also Hlaváček. He shook hands with the latter unenthusiastically, but Marie played her role perfectly. While the Gestapo watched, she kissed him pro forma as she would an estranged husband, but in her dancing eyes he could see the delight in seeing him alive. He also saw total confidence that whatever came next they would be able to deal with it.

In Prague they were brought inside the Gestapo headquarters at the former Peček Palace, named after a Jewish banker's family that was now living in the U.S. They were handled briskly but on the whole decently, with Leimer advising the surprised Krajina that he should tell K.H. Frank openly what he thought of the Nazi regime. Through his control of all police forces now that *Reichsprotektor* Heydrich was dead, Frank had become the de facto ruler of the Czech Protectorate. Of course there was still his boss, Deputy *Reichsprotektor* Daluege, but only formally. Before Krajina was to meet with them both, he was interrogated by Dr. Ernst Gerke, chief of the Prague Gestapo. Gerke's job was obviously to soften him up.

To test Krajina's thinking, Gerke suggested that Frank was about to offer him an important post in the puppet Czech Protectorate government. When Krajina stated unequivocally that he would never accept any such position, Gerke's manner became less civil. He was now obviously dealing with just another Czech prisoner. Perhaps a bit more important one, but still a prisoner.

At three o'clock in the afternoon, Leimer brought the tired and ailing Krajina into the official hall with its red velvet furnishings. There he found both Frank and Daluege, along with an interpreter, two secretaries and several other people. What followed was an unusual procedure. Frank, addressing Krajina formally by his university title as *Herr Dozent*, asked him to sign a piece of paper, which a graphic expert compared with Krajina's previous signature.

Once his identity was definitely established, Frank stood up, and with a broad smile officially offered Krajina "a high position or even a ministerial post in the Protectorate government." Again the recalcitrant Krajina lost no time in answering *Niemals mit Ihnen!* In other words: never with you.

Frank too then lost his smile, pronouncing him his prisoner. He asked him to summarize his political beliefs, and when Krajina answered that they were the same as those of President Beneš, Frank interrupted him to ask when he joined the Resistance. Because he knew the Gestapo would want to know the details, Krajina lied with alacrity, saying it was after November 1939, adding that in effect the Germans had caused the

Resistance to come into being by closing the universities. Denying a nation its cultural heritage meant challenging it to resist.

When the now annoyed Frank asked him who brought him into the Resistance, Krajina answered that it was Prokop Drtina, a man who was now safely tucked away in London exile. Krajina then fearlessly listed the mistakes the Germans had made in the Protectorate. When Frank asked him about his opinion of the puppet Czech Protectorate government, Krajina — this time truthfully — replied that it couldn't be lower.

Frank then asked him specifically about the most hated member of the cabinet, the quisling and former Czech military officer Emanuel Moravec. Krajina said he was considered to be a military deserter, and therefore no one could have any confidence in him.

Frank must have liked the answer, for he asked why Krajina did not then accept his offer and thereby improve the standing of the Czech government. "Because then there wouldn't be the slightest difference between Moravec and me," Krajina answered.

Toward the end of the meeting, Frank asked, once again in a more conciliatory tone, what could be done to improve relations between the Czechs and Germans. Krajina suggested that Frank release all Czech and Slovak political prisoners and that then — perhaps — the Czechs could begin to think differently.

Frank responded by saying that under present conditions with German military setbacks this was impossible. Everyone would regard such a gesture as a sign of weakness. Perhaps, he added, it would be possible when the German armies were once again advancing. Then Frank reminded Krajina: "Don't ever forget that you are my prisoner. The agreement with Hlaváček I will honour, on condition that you will not try to make contact with your Resistance at home or abroad. Because you did not surrender but were captured, you will be interrogated. But only about those things you yourself did in the Resistance."

Krajina's next interrogation came two days later by a Gestapo man named Krupke who began with a two-hour boastful monologue about all the things the Gestapo had discovered about the ÚVOD resistance group. This was extremely helpful for Krajina in formulating the defence strategy for himself and his group.

For example, when he heard that my father, Jaroslav Drábek, had been arrested and sent to Auschwitz, he decided to name him as his close collaborator. It was a bold move which in the end saved my father's life. Father was recalled for interrogation from Auschwitz where he would have been certain to die soon.

At one point, while being led to an interrogation room, Krajina noticed in one of the Gestapo offices an arrested man who had been a radio operator. He was hunched over some coding papers, and Krajina immediately suspected that the Germans were trying to establish fake radio contact with London.

A terrible fatigue, probably a delayed reaction to his dramatic capture, coupled with a bad case of flu, eventually brought Krajina down

Jaroslav Drábek, father of the author and the man who brought Krajina into the Resistance. This is his bilingual identity card (German and Czech) for the Nazi Protectorate of Bohemia and Moravia.

in his prison at Peček Palace. While lying in his bed he came to the realization that he would eventually have to decide whether to honour Hlaváček's pact with the Gestapo: that in return for no one in Krajina's group being harmed, Krajina would not attempt to contact London from prison. Hlaváček, who was imprisoned in the same room, never ceased to stress that keeping the pact could be done via the principle of feeding the wolf and yet keeping the goat alive (the equivalent in English is "having your cake and eating it too").

While Krajina did not feel bound by any pact made with the murderous Gestapo, it was important to appear as if he was adhering to it because so many lives were at stake. He didn't trust the Germans, being convinced that in the end they would probably execute his entire group as dangerous witnesses. He also understood that the Germans had already tried to contact London with the captured radio operator. He told this to Hlaváček, who eventually began to doubt the validity of the agreement, too.

Once Krajina reached this decision, he freely lied to the interrogating Leimer and also took other actions. He arranged to get a message to Lojzička, a brave and resourceful servant girl who worked for a woman arrested with the Krajina group and who occasionally came to the Gestapo with clean laundry for her. With Lojzička's help, Krajina managed to smuggle out a message, and eventually London was warned of these German efforts. Lojzička was just as fearless in dealing with other totalitarians in a few years later when she helped with the Krajinas' escape from the Communists. More about that later.

Krajina continued to mislead Leimer, assuring him that ÚVOD had been finished by his arrest. In reality Krajina could think of more than ten other members of his group who were still at large and could be counted on to carry on the organization's work. There were also at least three men who, he hoped, were still alive and could operate a transmitter.

Krajina was twice asked by a special interrogator about his Resistance group's super-informant Thümmel, the interrogator at first referring to Thümmel by František, one of his cover names, and in no way suggesting that he was asking about a German spy. Because there had been no mention of František in Krajina's testimony, the interrogator asked if Krajina knew that František had been caught. Krajina said he wasn't aware of it. The interrogator then correctly identified him as Thümmel. Soon after, Krajina learned that it had been a certain Colonel Churavý from the military Resistance group who had once unwisely written Thümmel's name in his notebook, and thereby had helped to identify him. Krajina had the distinct feeling that his interrogator was quite impressed by the fact that the Czech resistance was able to reach informants this high in the Nazi hierarchy.

When the nineteen-page-long official record of Krajina's activity was complete, the Gestapo men protested that Krajina had provided them with nothing they didn't already know. Krajina defended himself, saying that after his arrest there was no member of ÚVOD who was still at large, so there was nothing more to tell. At the same time he was of course hoping that no one else would be discovered. But even if they were, he was prepared to claim they constituted new personnel he knew nothing about.

Eventually Krajina, his wife and the group associated with them were transferred to Terezin's Little Fortress concentration camp. Before the transfer took place, the Gestapo took Krajina on a walk through Prague. This was their favourite ploy with prominent prisoners: allowing them to walk about freely, then arresting for interrogation anyone who greeted them. Fortunately in Krajina's case no one approached him, and it was a rare opportunity to take a walk through springtime Prague among his beloved blossoming trees.

6

In Captivity II

TEREZÍN, OR IN GERMAN Theresienstadt, had been established as an Austro-Hungarian fortress town late in the 18th century, supposedly to be used against the Prussians. But when the Prussians in their new designation as Germans defeated the Austrians in 1866, they had simply bypassed Terezín.

In the 1940s the town of Terezín was ideally suited as a staging area for Jews destined for the Eastern death camps, but far worse conditions prevailed in the section of town called the Little Fortress. There the Nazis had established a special prison for people who had dared to oppose them, regardless of their race.

Krajina and the Hlaváček group arrived in Terezín in the spring of 1943 where, since February of that year, a special section had been prepared for them. The group was designated as *Ehrenhäftlinge KHF*, i.e., Honour Prisoners of Karl Hermann Frank. The two Krajinas, Hlaváček himself and his three colleagues were all supposedly included in the

The gate of the "Small Fortress" (*Kleine Festung*) at Terezín in which the Krajinas were held captive. The ironic banner translates as "Work Brings Freedom."

Hlaváček agreement. Krajina kept reminding Leimer that his wife had been in Ravensbrück only as a hostage and that she was to be freed upon his capture. Leimer balked, explaining that this was impossible since the released Marie could carry messages to the Resistance. On the other hand Leimer suggested that the Krajinas could be joined in the Little Fortress by their eight-year-old daughter Milena. They refused the suggestion. Milena was living with her grandmother and they certainly didn't want her growing up in prison.

Because they were placed in a special section which had formerly been a stall, they were spared witnessing some of the horrors of the rest of the Little Fortress concentration camp, where over two and half thousand people died during the war. But the last group of forty-nine men and three women were executed by the Gestapo early in May 1945 di-

A row of prison cells at Terezín.

rectly in front of their windows, despite countermanding orders from the local *Wehrmacht* detachment. Krajina had already been taken away to Prague at that time, but the horrified Marie watched the whole thing, and a year later testified about it at the trial of K.H. Frank.

Exhausting times came when the Gestapo began bringing to Terezín various captured Resistance members. Krajina had to face them while they were questioned. This, of course, required intense concentration on the part of the prisoners, lest they betray some information the Gestapo didn't yet have.

One such prisoner was my father, who had shortly before returned from Auschwitz and had been placed in the prison hospital in Prague. There he was being treated for an infection in his leg, which a sympathetic Czech doctor kept in an artificially festering state. It was hoped that a seriously ill man would not be sent back to the death camp.

As Krajina described the confrontation in Terezín that day, Drábek (who had been advised to deny everything by the now fully turncoat Gestapo man Gall), claimed he had never met Hlaváček. He also allowed that he may have met Krajina while hiking in the mountains before the war, but that was all. According to Krajina's later description, Drábek seemed angry with him because he had brought him into this precarious situation, but that must have been an act. Krajina, on the other hand, told the Gestapo that he was not angry with father who had always been too reluctant to join the Resistance. In other words, Krajina, as a ploy, was suggesting that father was a coward. In effect, Krajina, who had caused father to be brought back from Auschwitz, was reversing his earlier claim. Still, he must have sounded convincing because the Gestapo man Pfitsch, who had brought father over from Prague, started suspecting that there may have been something to what Krajina was saying. But since Pfitsch wasn't fully convinced, Krajina, for good measure, directed his next rather bold statement at him, saying that he found it strange the Gestapo was sending innocent cowards like Drábek to Auschwitz, thus hoping that such arrogant presumptuosness would create serious doubts about father's involvement in the Resistance.

Here's how father described that interrogation in his own memoir:

"That day in Terezín was quite tense. First to give testimony was Hlaváček, whom I immediately recognized, although I said I didn't know him. He claimed that occasionally we used to meet (which was true). Next came Krajina, who gave such vague testimony that Pfitsch was thoroughly confused and repeatedly threatened to have his agreement with the Gestapo invalidated since he was not telling the truth as promised. Despite the whole thing constituting a matter of life and death for us all, I almost had to laugh as I lay there on the stretcher.

"In the end Pfitsch grew tired of it all and had me carried to the courtyard. There poor Hlaváček sneaked up and in a whisper pleaded with me to forgive him. He said he had to admit to our meetings otherwise he would have threatened the validity of the agreement made with the Gestapo. He confessed that he was unable to break his word even to the Gestapo and in the end it was I who had to assure him that everything was okay and that I was not angry with him."

While it was still not certain whether the performance would save father from being returned to Auschwitz, another serious danger for the Krajina group arose. After several months spent trying to allay London's suspicions that they were no longer communicating with the Resistance but the Gestapo, the Germans gave up the pretense, and concluded that Krajina's group must have somehow managed to alert London.

In March 1944 Krajina was brought back to Prague for a far tougher interrogation about the the warning sent to London. This time Leimer started by telling Krajina that the agreement was now invalid and that he would have not only the entire Hlaváček group executed, but Krajina's immediate family as well, including his daughter and the mother-in-law with whom she lived. But he implied that the orders for execution might still be rescinded if Krajina confessed in detail how the warning sent to London had been accomplished.

Other Gestapo men joined Leimer to hear Krajina's answer. He calmly pointed out that London could probably detect that the transmitter was being operated by someone else by the very touch of the Morse code operator, but that didn't make much of an impression, and the interrogation became more intense. The window was opened and the heating turned off. At that point Krajina noticed that there were no bars on the window and he contemplated suicide, but decided that it could have been construed as a de facto confession and that the threat to his group and family could be carried out. He decided to fight, continuing to deny everything. He recalled the event later: "Towards morning even in the unbearable cold I began to fall asleep. They took my coat off and through a hose kept spraying me with water which nearly froze on my body. They didn't beat me, on that point they were still honouring the agreement. In the evening I was sent to my cell at Pankrác while advising me to think about it and to ask for some paper when I wanted to write down a confession."

Instead of asking for writing impliments, Krajina remained recalcitrant. All prisoners were ordered to stand at attention and to rattle off the number of their cell and their names whenever the window to their cell was opened. Krajina flatly refused, claiming he had the status of a Prisoner of Honour and that it was not required of such detainees.

Several things saved Krajina's life this time. One was that to K.H. Frank he was still more valuable alive. Another was that the detection by London could have been possible through technical means. But by far the most convincing proof of Krajina's innocence was Frank's arrogant speech in Prague which was carried across the Protectorate by radio. In it he boasted about the capture of the parachutists and their transmitter by the Gestapo. Krajina found out about this speech and told Leimer that London had doubtlessly heard about it as well. "That was idiotic!" Leimer exclaimed when he heard about Frank's boasting.

Krajina was eventually returned to Terezín where he became instrumental in my father's release from prison. It happened this way: when Gall, the turncoat Gestapo man, was caught trying to smuggle into Prague some black market food from the countryside, he was sent for a few days to a special detention for Germans in Terezín. Doing his best to give the impression of a good Gestapo man, Gall asked to be kept busy by preparing a report on Krajina in relation to Drábek.

The problem was how to convince Krajina that Gall was really a turncoat who could be trusted. It was my mother who came to the rescue, remembering that Krajina loved a certain type of ginger cookies. She baked a box of them, which Gall took with him to Terezín. Recognizing who had baked the cookies, Krajina realized that they signalled Gall was to be trusted. Krajina then accepted Gall and the two men concocted a report about my father which totally exonerated him.

In the summer of that year the Gestapo chief of the Little Fortress decided to make use of the botanist Krajina and ordered him to build a rock garden. Although Krajina enjoyed being outdoors in the fresh air, he was not allowed any helpers and was forced to transport heavy stones in a wheelbarrow all by himself. Each night after such toil he returned to his cell exhausted.

There were, nevertheless, many encouraging signs. That spring the Allies landed in Normandy, and in the summer came the attempt on Hitler's life. Unsuccessful though it was, it gave hope that there was resistance within Hitler's close associates. Less encouraging was Hitler's subsequent statement that he saw in his survival a sign of Providence to continue with his task. But shortly afterwards, Paris and Florence fell, and on the Eastern front the Red Army stood before Warsaw. It was obvious that the Allies were continuing with their push to the East and the long struggle up through Italy.

That summer Leimer, who had been stationed in Prague, returned to Terezín. Referring to the unsuccessful Gestapo attempts to establish radio contact with London, he mentioned that he was still sure that Krajina must have had a hand it. It was obvious that Leimer found it difficult to admit he had been unsuccesful in pinning the guilt on him. Leimer also warned Krajina not to attempt to make contact with other prisoners, probably suspecting an uprising in the now poorly guarded Terezín. "It's important for me that you stay alive and healthy until the end of the war. I have a plan which involves you," he uttered mysteriously, without giving the slightest explanation of what he meant.

The following day news came that my father had been released from prison. Krajina could chalk up another victory.

7

Surviving

IN THE MIDDLE of April 1945, a further grave danger arose in Terezín when a group of prisoners was ordered to begin digging a wide trench. They were ordered to work day and night. Although strictly forbidden to do so, Krajina who was working nearby on his rock garden, climbed to the top of the ramparts and immediately recognized the makings of a mass grave. Heinrich Jöckl, the commandant of the Little Fortress, wanted to make sure no witnesses would remain to testify about his reign of terror. Krajina surmised that the mass execution of some seven hundred prisoners was about to begin. Honour prisoners or not, he had no doubt that his group would be included.

Most of the prisoners — although not all — were saved in the nick of time by the arrival of the *Wehrmacht* General Neumann, commander of the military area around Terezín. After a sharp exchange with Jöckl, he countermanded the execution orders, telling the commandant that, as it was, all Germans would have to suffer for the crimes committed by the Gestapo. It was madness to add others.

That was on April 28, 1945. Three days later, early in the morning, Krajina was awakened in his cell at the Little Fortress. He was shaved and his hair was cut before being fitted in a car among four Gestapo men and driven to Prague. As they were departing they told his wife, with the usual dose of Gestapo-style sarcasm, that she should start looking for a new husband.

On the way to Prague, Krajina noticed that some of the flags with swastikas on them were hanging at half-mast and wondered why. He didn't yet know that Hitler had committed suicide. The accompanying Gestapo men were not about to tell him, although he was aware that the Czech exile government was already in Slovakia. That last bit of news filled him with optimism, despite the fact that the men around him might have been taking him to his execution. He also felt positive about the fact that condemned men were not as a rule given a haircut and a shave by the Gestapo.

A bit of gallows humour was added to the trip, Krajina felt, when some of the Czechs who saw a car passing with Nazi uniforms inside shook their fists at them. In Prague he was escorted inside the Gestapo headquarters by a man so drunk he tripped several times going up the steps to the Peček Palace. That once again caused Krajina to look around for a means of escape, but the main entrance was still guarded by men who seemed alert.

Delivering him to the same red-velvet-lined room where two years before he had been interrogated by K.H. Frank himself, the drunken Gestapo man merrily informed Krajina that he should already be dead because his name was at the top of the seven hundred prisoners scheduled to be executed at the Little Fortress. Then he left.

After a half hour alone, Krajina quietly opened the door and found that there were many other Gestapo men around, most in various states of inebriation. He also noted, however, that he was still a closely watched individual.

In another half hour the door flew open and Leimer appeared — the same Leimer who had arrested him two years before and who had interrogated him so many times since. In what seemed to be under the circumstances a comical manner, Leimer saluted and reported something so quickly that Krajina found it largely unintelligible. It sounded as if he were addressing his superior.

Finally Krajina began to understand that Leimer was surrendering to him since, as he reported, the Czechs had won. Leimer expected Krajina would now become a prominent political personage who would want to confer with K.H. Frank to prevent further bloodshed. According to Leimer, Frank was already speaking with other Czechs in an effort to negotiate a truce which would enable the German forces to move westward where they could surrender to the Americans. This was preferable to surrendering to the Russians, who frequently didn't adhere to the rule of law when it came to the Gestapo and the SS.

Krajina asked Leimer to relax and sit down. Then he informed him that he agreed with him: for the Germans the war was lost. Unfortunately this was the only thing on which they agreed. He was refusing to become Leimer's superior, and he was also refusing to talk with Frank. The reason for this was simple: Frank was now no partner for any of the Czechs but a war criminal. Krajina was equally adamant in refusing to join any newly formed Czechoslovak collaborationist government because the exile government was no longer exiled but already on Czechoslovak territory in Slovakia. If he joined anyone, it would be that particular government. It certainly would not be the Germans. He grew bolder as he spoke, recognizing that his refusal to cooperate with K.H. Frank might result in his death, but also concluding that he would prefer that to being shot later by the Czechs for collaborating with the enemy.

After hearing this, Leimer practically collapsed, saying that Krajina could save many lives by cooperating. He then talked for some time, trying to make Krajina change his mind. Toward evening, Leimer informed Krajina that due to his refusal to cooperate, he could not be released and that he would be interned near Prague. But he promised that his wife and others from the group would be freed. Krajina was taken to a castle called Jenerálka in the middle of Šárka, a large park on the city's outskirts. When Krajina found out the names of other *Pro-*

Jenerálka Castle in Prague where Krajina was interned
during the last days of World War II.

minenten interned there, he realized he knew practically all of them personally.

Each morning the German commandant of Jenerálka came to his cell to ask if he had changed his mind, and when Krajina informed him that he hadn't, he left again abruptly, slamming the door behind him.

On May 4th, Marie arrived with a change of clothes, and Krajina knew she had indeed been freed. She indicated to him that plans were being made for him to be liberated as well. The following day Leimer visited him, once more asking if he had changed his mind because he was just on his way to see Frank that morning. By then the houses around Jenerálka were already decorated with Czechoslovak flags, although the swastika still hung on the prison building itself, where the guards were fully armed and on continuous alert.

The end of his imprisonment came two days later when Leimer entered Krajina's cell once more, this time with a member of the Czech Revolutionary Council, and asked Krajina to take part in the peace negotiations. This time Krajina relented but only after he negotiated the release of all Czech prisoners at Jenerálka. Then they marched under a white flag through a Prague that now was full of barricades. The uprising was in full swing.

"Along the way we were greeted by many armed and unarmed revolutionaries. But we were unable to take in the scene fully because our eyes were filled with tears. They were those of happiness as well as sadness for the many brave warriors who had not lived to see this day," Krajina remembered.

At the nearest Czech military post they discovered that the German army had already capitulated, which alleviated the need for any further negotiations. Krajina had then given Leimer, who had been walking apathetically alongside the group, a choice: either return and join the remaining German forces at Jenerálka, or surrender to the Czechs on the spot and help by giving them useful information about the Gestapo. In the end Leimer chose to surrender to the Czechs, and Krajina handed him over to the revolutionaries, at the same time telling him the truth that there was no way he could guarantee his life. The circle had been closed. Krajina had arrested the man who two years earlier had arrested him.

There has been much subsequent speculation about Leimer's fate. According to Soviet sources he was executed two years later, but there are some who doubt it. His extensive knowledge of the workings of the Gestapo made him too valuable. He may also have been a double agent, as there were reports that he had lived for years afterwards in East Germany.

Even after the capitulation of the German army, the dangerous times were not quite over for Krajina as he again dodged bullets to help arrange the surrender of a German machine gun nest at a nearby school. It produced valuable automatic weapons along with ammunition for the revolutionaries. For two more days there would still be fighting on Prague's streets.

Then the Red Army entered the Czech capital, which by then had pretty much liberated itself with the help of the turncoat Russian troops of General Vlasov, who had earlier been outfitted by the Nazis to fight against Stalin on the Eastern Front. But here in Prague, Vlasov once more changed his allegiance and helped the Czechs against the Nazis. Stalin never forgave Vlasov for this, and he and his units were rounded up by the Red Army. Vlasov was executed a year later along with his officers and most of his men; the rest were sent into Siberian exile. Those who were wounded were shot and killed while still in their Prague hospital beds.

The fighting over, my father "liberated" two apartments in our building, heretofore occupied by Germans who had either been interned or had fled. Later, father, with his tongue firmly in his cheek, explained this was done while "espousing the confiscatory laws of the revolution." Whatever the legal basis, Krajina with Marie immediately moved into one of the apartments, soon to be joined by their daughter Milena along with Marie's mother who had been caring for her.

Those were immensely heady days. In the full bloom of a Prague spring, the city was filled with units of the liberating armies. Before the end of May the once exiled Czechoslovak government returned; a few days later President Beneš was welcomed by thousands as his train slowly made its way to Prague from the East. The Czechoslovak exiles that formed contingents within the Red and the British Armies arrived for a parade and were cheered by crowds frenzied with adulation. General Eisenhower, Field Marshal Montgomery and the Soviet Marshal Konev came to be thanked personally. The Czechs were introduced to Hershey bars, Juicy Fruit chewing gum and canned orange juice. Frequently there was spontaneous dancing. Boy Scout uniforms and those of the Czech patriotic Sokols — both organizations forbidden by the Nazis — appeared in profusion in the streets as young people tried to learn the strange words to "Chattanooga Choo Choo."

There were also much more sombre moments when transports of emaciated prisoners arrived from the liberated concentration camps with sad news about those who would never come back. Gradually the newspapers began to write about those in the Resistance who had survived, and there was general astonishment over what had been accomplished by the Czechs in providing information for the Allies.

Karl Hermann Frank was captured by the Americans in Germany.

To his great surprise he was not treated as a prisoner of war who merely followed orders (as he had supposed), but as a war criminal. That was certainly the way Vladimír Krajina and the vast majority of Czechs saw him.

Krajina himself was practically unknown. Curiously enough, it was Frank himself who introduced his name to the Czech press after his own capture by referring to him as the leader of the Czech Resistance. Since Frank's reference was verbal and not written out, the Communist-controlled *Mladá fronta* newspaper mistook his name and kept referring to him as "Kraina."

The Communists had no heroes of Krajina's calibre or achievements in the Resistance. There was a man named Fučík, but his achievements were mediocre by comparison. Also, there was strong suspicion that, if he had not actually consciously collaborated with the Gestapo, he had possibly helped it, at least through his naïveté. An unfortunate Communist journalist, he had not yet been fully developed into a hero; that would take more time, effort and retouching. It was also rumoured that his book, *Reportáž psaná na oprátce* (Report from the Gallows), was edited after the war for propaganda purposes by Communist Party experts.

So far as their propaganda was concerned, the Soviet-backed Communists had to cope with another handicap: this was that until the German attack in the summer of 1941, their hands had often been tied by the Nazi-Soviet Pact. Although after the start of the war the Soviet losses were horrendous on the Eastern front, it was during those two initial years before the German attack on Russia that the democratic Resistance, with Krajina in the forefront, registered its greatest successes. The Communist propaganda also had to answer for the revolt of its sympathizers within the ranks of the Czechoslovak exile army in England: until the Nazi invasion they considered World War II to be a "bourgeois" war and wanted no part of it.

But Fučík's biggest handicap for the Communists was that he was dead: he had been hanged by the Nazis in 1943. Martyrs were fine so far as they went, but Fučík's life had ended two years ago, while Krajina was a living, breathing and ready-made hero. There was no need to edit his story, and the Communists soon approached him with offers of a high position should he join them.

There was no chance of that. His Christian upbringing and his devotion to the democratic principles stood firmly in the way. These principles were symbolized by the gold watch he had once received from President Masaryk, and now by the triumphant return of his personal hero — the victorious President Beneš. In any case, Krajina was not dreaming of a political career. He longed to return to his herbaria.

Like Ferdinand the Bull, he simply wanted to pause and smell the flowers.

8

False Beginnings

IF VLADIMIR KRAJINA thought that he would be able to return to his flowers at the war's end, he was sadly mistaken. Political problems soon developed that were, for the home Resistance, totally unexpected. Basically they all stemmed from the fact that the Red Army now occupied most of the country. Although it was not entirely true, the Communist propaganda machine never let the Czechs forget that it was the Soviets who liberated Prague, not the Western Allies. For good measure, the Communists reminded them that it was the Western Allies who had engineered the disastrous Munich Agreement of 1938, while carefully omitting any reference to the Nazi-Soviet Pact signed the following year. Their plan for the domination of Czechoslovakia entailed taking over the country without the use of the military: in other words, using the democratic system to their own advantage.

There is a story about General Patton, whose Third Army reached as far as the Czech town of Plzeň (Pilsen), which is eighty-eight kilo-

SW

metres east of Prague. Eisenhower, as the Supreme Allied Commander, explained to Patton that there was an agreement with the Russians that they would be allowed to enter Prague first. According to the story, Patton suggested that Eisenhower did not have to know anything about how far the Third Army had advanced until he got a call from Patton from a telephone booth on Wenceslas Square. Whereupon, again according to the story, Eisenhower gave him strict orders not to move beyond the agreed on Plzeň-Karlovy Vary (Pilsen-Karlsbad) line. The story may well be apocryphal but accurate to the degree that Patton and Eisenhower often espoused different approaches.

In May 1945 Eisenhower no longer considered Prague militarily important. In this he was, of course, correct. The problem with military men is that at least some of them do not quite understand the concept of *political* importance.

President Beneš' return may have been triumphant, but it was also costly. It had to be achieved via Moscow, and Beneš had to close his eyes to the brazen Soviet annexation of Subcarpathian Ukraine, which had been part of pre-war Czechoslovakia. Under Communist pressure, Beneš also reneged on his promise to replace several ministers in the cabinet by home Resistance people who were not Communists. All of that added to Communist influence and increased the need for a strong showing by the democratic parties in the next election.

Another of my father's good friends, Prokop Drtina, was now back from his London exile. He was a hero, widely known for his immensely popular broadcasts over the BBC. He lost no time informing those from his Resistance group who had survived about all these new challenges from the Communist side.

Soon after the liberation in May, Krajina and his wife made a brief visit to his native Moravia. He boldly commandeered a train engine and, bored by the three-hour ride, even helped to shovel the coal. According to a family story, he arrived there — at least so far as his appearance was concerned — in a darkened state. He had time to spend just a few hours with his elderly mother, almost immediately returning to Prague aboard the same engine. His wife caught a ride aboard a truck the next day.

Those were the magic days in immediate post-war Czechoslovakia,

Resistance members welcoming their colleague Prokop Drtina from
London exile at a Prague Airport, May 1945. (Note the Red Army soldiers
on a tank in the background.) FROM LEFT TO RIGHT: Rudolf Jilovský,
Vladimír Krajina, Prokop Drtina, Jaroslav Drábek, Arnošt Heidrich.

which was one of the victorious Allies. Everything seemed to be coming
up roses. It was May, nature was in full bloom, Hitler was dead and Germany on its knees. That summer at the Potsdam Conference, the Allies
would put their stamp of approval on the expulsion of three million
Germans from the country and — as the Czechs saw it — everything

would be set right again. With a historical perspective, such feelings may now seem somewhat naïve, but it's a good thing that humankind does not have the advantage of an immediate historical perspective. Otherwise there would probably be little joy in living.

Back in Prague the enthusiastic Krajina plunged into a major project for the democrats — setting up an organization of all Resistance members to ensure their rights were not trampled on in the newly restored republic. But already then he saw that the Communists were expert strategists. It was thought that Krajina was a natural for the presidency of the organization. The Communists, however, knowing that they couldn't come up with a Marxist candidate with comparable credentials, managed to bring in a highly malleable left-wing Social Democrat through whom they would gradually take control of the organization.

And not only that, the Communist Party's General Secretary Rudolf Slánský (whom his own party would later murder on orders from Stalin), managed successfully to promote the name of the organization as the Association of the National Revolution. Drtina noted that this was a genuine travesty since the Resistance effort had nothing to do with a revolution (which was, of course, a popular Marxist concept), but with restitution, in other words, restoring the democratic republic of Czechoslovakia.

These defeats further convinced Krajina that his idea of returning exclusively to his flowers had been a pipe dream. In August of 1945 Drtina asked Krajina to accompany him on a political tour of Moravia on behalf of the Czech National Socialist Party. At the Moravian town of Olomouc, the local party functionaries told Krajina how those who had profited during the war were now joining the Communist Party en masse — after being promised by its functionaries that all would be forgiven.

And it was not only the collaborationists and profiteers who were being recruited into the Communist ranks. Former members of the conservative Agrarian Party were threatened with prosecution by the Communist-controlled regional courts should they not join.

After these revelations Krajina would not have been true to his principles had he not decided to go into politics. Although entering the political area appealed to his sense of justice, at home he had his hands full with convincing Marie that he should actively join in the struggle. He insisted that he and she, veterans of Nazi prisons, must not cross the road and side with "the careful ones," in other words, must not stay out of trouble. Although at times he was criticized for his pessimistic view of the situation, Krajina believed that the final battle between the democrats and the totalitarians was not far off and that it wasn't at all certain who would emerge victorious.

He was also preparing to resume his lectures at the newly reopened Charles University, but that too was preceded by his accepting the presidency of the university's cleansing committee. Three professors were brought before it, accused of collaborating with the Nazis. One of them was Krajina's former adversarial boss, Professor Domin. But there was no vengeance: in the end, all three were pardoned.

In the fall of 1945 Prokop Drtina, heretofore a secretary to President Beneš, was named Minister of Justice, representing the Czech National Socialists in one of the cabinet's most important posts. Altogether there were four Czech National Socialists in the cabinet, they hoped their numbers would increase even further once some of the Communists' nefarious practices were exposed.

For that, however, they needed to be well organized. What they lacked at the moment was an architect for such organization — a general secretary, who would be the highest executive officer of the party. One old party stalwart seemed to be an obvious choice, except that his health was so seriously undermined he was forced to decline the post. Someone else had to be found, and quickly.

The leading Czech Communists who had been in a Moscow exile returned, not only with an experienced general secretary but also with a well-developed program. They semed much better prepared for the post-war uncertainty and downright chaos that was providing them with unique opportunities for a government takeover. National elections were called for in May 1946, and the Czech National Socialists, generally considered the strongest of the democratic parties, were under increased pressure to come up with a program that would thwart such a takeover. That, of course, included finding a capable general secretary.

It was the somewhat desperate Czech National Socialist leader Zenkl who told Drtina that a group of Czech National Socialists had recently discussed appointing Krajina to the post. Drtina knew Krajina well from the early days of the Resistance because he had worked with him closely. As has been mentioned, a few weeks earlier, he had also made a political tour with Krajina across Moravia. Although Drtina was a great admirer of Krajina, he was somewhat taken aback by the proposal.

In Drtina's reply to the party leader Zenkl, he praised Krajina as an outstanding worker with great energy and a man whose political thinking was certainly in the spirit of the Czech National Socialists. He stated Krajina's principles were firm and unwavering, also that he was exceptionally brave, as he had proven again and again during the war. But according to Drtina, Krajina had no experience in political life. He did not know the structure of the party well, nor most of the people in it. In short, he was something of a neophyte when it came to politics.

In the end, however, Drtina decided not to oppose Krajina's appointment, justifying it as follows: "I was thoroughly convinced of his personal devotion to me and I knew that from that standpoint I could not depend in that function on anyone else more completely than him. . . . I was convinced that in Krajina's possible appointment Zenkl saw as clearly as I did that this particular general secretary would have neither interest nor personal characteristics . . . which would cause him to misuse his position for intrigues against the chairman of the party."

Krajina, of course, had no idea that Drtina was initially against his appointment. He didn't find out until he read about it in Drtina's memoirs, first published in 1982 in Toronto. In his own reminiscences, Krajina mentions that after having toured Moravia with Drtina, political life attracted him more and more. He also writes, however, that had he known Drtina was initially against his appointment as general secretary, he would never have accepted the post.

But accept it he did, and thereby Krajina's fate was sealed. It may be possible to imagine him immersing himself exclusively in his beloved botany, concentrating on sorting and smelling the flowers in his herbarium. It is not likely, however, that such a life would have lasted long. The totalitarian restrictions on foreign travel and free exchange of ideas would have soon engendered his resentment, which in the past had resulted in direct action. In addition, his close friendship with the democratically minded Resistance members during and after the war would have made the Communists highly suspicious of him.

Moreover, Krajina could not have stood idly by and watched what was going on all around him: the country's immediate post-war optimism subdued with the renewal of oppression, concentration camps and judicial murders. He would not have been able to watch his children growing up in the midst of officially sanctioned lies by a country for which he had just a few years earlier risked his life again and again.

Consequently, he accepted the post of general secretary with all its serious challenges. Among his first assignments was to tell two old-time party members that, because of their wartime unreliability, the party would not put them on its list of candidates for a parliamentary seat. One of them received a consolation prize by being named the presiding judge of the Supreme Court, but this still wasn't enough for him because, as Krajina succinctly put it in his reminiscences, "his smugness was boundless." Eventually the man signed up with the Communists.

The second person he had to inform was more interesting, Emanuel Šlechta, an ambitious and prominent Czech National Socialist party member. Šlechta's wife was known to have associated with Gestapo men, supposedly to save her imprisoned husband. Since the Communists knew about this and were likely to make it public when it suited them most — possibly even use it for blackmail — her husband was a liability and therefore rejected as a candidate.

Krajina gave Šlechta the news in the afternoon. That evening at a grand ball of the young Czech National Socialists, during a ladies' choice, Krajina was asked to dance by an unknown attractive woman. While dancing, she told him that she was Šlechta's wife and asked to see him in his office the next day. There she admitted that she had indeed had affairs with Gestapo men and that there had been many more than one, but at the same time said that this was not a reason for her husband to be punished. Krajina interrupted her flirtatious eloquence to thank her for confirming the information he already had, but this only hardened his conviction that Šlechta should not be a candidate. The ever-ambitious Šlechta also became a Communist stooge as a result.

On the other hand, in his position Krajina tried to entice Václav Černý, the literary and philosophical giant, to be a candidate. Černý declined, explaining that the political orientation of the Czech National Socialists was too far to the right for his taste.

⟨⟩

Černý is important to the Krajina story in another way. His memoir, entitled *Pláč koruny české* (The Weeping of the Czech Crown), published in 1977 by the exile Sixty-Eight Publishers in Toronto, is not only thoroughly enlightening as to the mechanics of the activities of the Resistance but also a valuable piece of Czech literature

Černý noted that from the year 1940 on, there had been criticism of Krajina's dominant role in transmitting intelligence to London, to the effect that Krajina had "autocratic tendencies," that he was too selective in choosing which items should be transmitted. Also that he formulated them too much in his own style, at the same time arbitrarily deciding on their significance, that he tried to make it appear as if he himself was the source, when in fact they were the result of an entire network of active informants.

This criticism came from other Resistance groups as well, especially the military one, the Defence of the Nation. At one point, the group went so far as to obtain its own transmitter, Sparta II, so that the home military Resistance group would be independent of Krajina.

"Dear reader," wrote Černý, "accept all that about Krajina as the truth, but do not overestimate the significance of this truth; or at least break off the point of that personal polemical barb."

It would be too bad, according to Černý's defence of Krajina, if the one who personally assumed the deadly risk of transmitting did not have the right to assess the material, to select from it according to its real significance, even to tame its vehemence sometimes and also its naïvely polemical edge. Černý points out that the military underground group, with their Sparta II, later did the very thing of which they accused Krajina.

Černý writes that it was, after all, a living person who chose the material to be transmitted and that this person was guided mainly by security considerations. Aside from objective necessities, such a person was also quite naturally influenced by his own views.

As to the origin of the messages, according to Černý it was not important that London knew who was the source; the main thing was that it was receiving them. Černý adds that in London at times they were also receiving messages supplied by himself personally, but Černý was not in the slightest interested in seeing his name or pseudonym survive in some Resistance archive after the war. The only thing that mattered was that he was able to channel his news to the transmitter. Nothing else was really his business.

Still, according to Černý's assessment, Krajina was not always averse to collaborating with Communists "as long as he could trust them." Černý admits he — Černý — was personally opposed to such collaboration. As his justification, he quotes from article three of the Nazi-Soviet pact in which both countries wish the re-instatement of peace, and call upon Britain and France to stop their "senseless and hopeless" war with Germany.

"Krajina," according to Černý, "was a man with straightforward thinking who didn't like to alter the conclusions he had arrived at. He was stubborn, not at all a tactician. And, as is usually the case with people who are not tacticians, he insisted on discipline that much more."

Černý concluded that despite Krajina's willingness to work with the Communists, he never overcame his suspicion that in their Resistance work they were guided by their own party's special post-war ideological goals. To them, these always came first. Krajina, on the other hand, never intended to subordinate his exclusive goal of national liberation to anything else. Further, in dealing with the Communists, he sensed a heightened danger of betrayal. In fact he was convinced that the Communist underground organization was unusually prone to betrayal. Despite all this, he was not averse to collaborating with them when the occasion warranted it, when the stakes were high enough.

Černý valued Krajina over those who were mere planners rather than warriors — those, as Černý explained, who in the seclusion of their own libraries kept thinking up *better reasons* for others to risk their necks.

"I used to say to myself," reminisces Černý in his memoirs, "that during the years 1939–1945 our cultural intelligentsia had acquired a moral legitimacy. . . . There was no doubt in my mind it was this group which alone had the right to talk about our national and state future. Of course on condition that this group, which had such strong will to suffer, resist and fight, at the moment of liberation will eject from its midst that meagre infection of a handful of traitors, cowards and swindlers. The percentage of fallen writers and those who belonged to the intelligentsia was in our Resistance fantastically higher than in any other European Resistance movement. One's astonishment at their number knows no bounds. . . ."

Černý saw his own war years in the Resistance as a personal adventure. As he says, "At the same time it was a test of character, it offered one a superb opportunity for self realization and self formulation. And thereby it brought me personally into the closest relationshiop with dear friends, valued above all others. And through the fact that common work such as ours, which constituted common risks as well, friends meet and are drawn together exclusively by that which is best in them. . . ."

At this point in his memoir Černý names nine Resistance leaders — among them Krajina — calling them his unforgettable friends. Then he addresses them personally: "That I have been allowed to live with you I shall remain grateful until I die. My fate could not have been better. On account of my memories of the six years alongside you I have written this belated memoir. . . . When an unknown Czech child asks who it was, let everyone truthfully answer: My child, this was a MAN!"

Among those names Černý lists, all but Krajina were his writing friends that he knew as an editor of an influential literary magazine. Krajina was the only one not engaged in humanities and also the only one whom he did not know before the war.

It may be argued that Černý's stress on the achievements of the Czech intelligentsia may be, if not downright self-serving, a bit restrictive due to his own narrow focus as an exceptionally learned man. This could be in reaction to the rampant post-war Communist propaganda at the time he wrote this, which did not allow in its version of history for any other significant World War II Resistance activity but that of its own cells. Also because Černý was a member of a generation which saw the birth of the Czechoslovak Republic in 1918 to be largely the work of university professors and the intelligentsia.

In the end of his section dealing with Krajina, Černý admitted he himself made serious mistakes of judgement. During the war, Černý, for example, insisted on drawing "a fanatically precise picture of the national future for himself." But one thing Černý claims he was never guilty of: while he was a radical and an intellectual he, like Krajina, took great care never to allow his personal views to disrupt the discipline of the Resistance movement. Athough they did not always agree with those above them, in the end both Krajina and Černý were soldiers, following orders from those above.

⟡

The academic year for the autumn of 1945 began with Krajina managing to make his students uncomfortable by scheduling his lectures early in the morning because of other commitments later in the day. Although he accepted no pay for the position of general secretary, he suddenly found himself a part of the leadership of the strongest anti-Communist party, with all the demands on his time this entailed. In addition, there was his appointment as a deputy in the National Constitutional Assembly, and the following May, at election time, his duties increased with his being elected a member of parliament. There was, however, disappointment connected with it. The Communists had won the first postwar election, and they would ensure that the election would be the only democratic election for the next forty-four years. The Communists' share of votes in the Czech lands was over 40 percent, with the Czech National Socialists in second place with 24 percent. It was not yet a complete takeover of power, but the Communist influence was greatly increased.

The result surprised even the Communists themselves. Playing the Red Army liberation card, using intimidation and blackmail, and pointing out the West's supposedly treasonable actions in Munich in 1938, they found that these strategies worked even better than they had expected, although only in the Czech lands. In Slovakia the Communists were dealt a resounding defeat. But Prague — along with the majority of the population — was in the Czech lands and that's where the major decisions were made.

The Krajinas were now living in their Kročínova Street apartment in the centre of Prague, with daughter Milena attending school nearby, but there were problems. In 1946 Marie, still weakened by her many years of imprisonment, lost her newborn child. Athough she almost died in the process of giving birth, she and Vladimir decided that they wanted another child. Late the following year, her son Vladimír junior was born. It was a difficult birth and her loss of blood was so dramatic that her gynecologist, impressed by her personal history and that of her husband, lay down on the bed next to her and donated to her directly a pint of his own blood. Such gestures towards those who had sacrificed so much for the country were still common then.

With Krajina's ascension into a politically prominent position, there were steadily increasing rumours in the Communist press about Krajina's supposed collaboration with K.H. Frank and the Nazis. The Communists believed his reputation as a Resistance hero needed to be dramatically tarnished. After an unsuccessful meeting with the Communist ministers of the Interior and Information, Krajina insisted on the creation of a ministerial commission to investigate his wartime activities.

Krajina's testimony before the committee consisted of 177 pages. Although it was chaired by a Communist, the overwhelming evidence in Krajina's favour eventually forced the committee to issue a statement, concluding that "the suspicions against Docent Krajina, which had been originally created, were through subsequent proceedings in all their aspects completely dispersed." Perhaps it wasn't the best syntax available, but for Krajina it was sufficient. He was cleared.

Or so he thought. Enter Major Pokorný, whose entrance was definitely from the left. This officer, who was in the employ of the Communist Ministry of the Interior, gained entry to the top SS man, Karl Hermann Frank, in his prison cell to interrogate him about Krajina. Pokorný then produced a record of the interrogation in Czech, a language which Frank never mastered. Pokorný verbally summarized its contents for Frank in German, and Frank reluctantly signed it. But

The Krajinas shortly after the birth of their son, Vlad Jr., 1947.

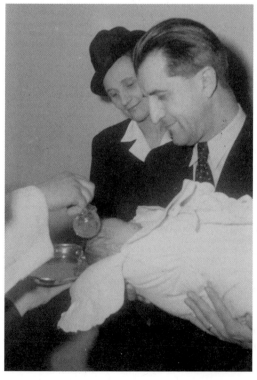

The Krajinas at the
christening of their son, 1947.

being an old master of lies and subterfuge himself, Frank became suspicious. He immediately sat down and made notes about what he had said. Then he reported Major Pokorný's visit to the state's attorney who had been appointed by Justice Minister Drtina.

Pokorný's report was compared with Frank's notes. It was found that in the former Frank had accused Krajina of having betrayed the parachutists in the Czech Paradise region in 1943; also that Krajina had been sent by Frank to the Jenerálka in 1945 because Krajina was collaborating with the Gestapo and had accepted a post in the Protectorate government. In Frank's notes there was no mention of either of those points. On the contrary, Krajina's heroism in resisting the Germans was described in glowing terms.

In his description of his meeting with Frank to discuss the Krajina protocol, the state's attorney noticed an expression on Frank's face, which he read as something to the effect, "we told you so about the Bolsheviks but you would not listen . . . ," and he notes how he resented being shamed by this Nazi with so much blood on his hands.

It wasn't difficult to disprove the allegations in Pokorný's version of the Frank protocol. The parachutists had been captured *before* Krajina was, so how could he have betrayed them to the Gestapo? And it wasn't only Krajina that had been brought to Jenerálka, but six other men as well, none of them having any idea why. When they were finally told, all of them refused to cooperate with the Germans.

Minister Drtina brought the matter up in the cabinet and demanded that Major Pokorný be fired. The Communists refused to go that far, but they did transfer him to Slovakia, out of harm's way. Twenty-two years later, during the Prague Spring, Major Pokorný was found hanging from a tree in a Moravian forest. There were strong suspicions that this was not suicide, as it had been presented, but a way at a time of liberalization for the hardline Communists to get rid of a potentially damaging witness to their crimes.

While Krajina managed to defend himself successfully against Communist onslaughts several times during this immediate post-war period, the country as a whole was not as fortunate. A serious blow to its independence came in the summer of 1947, when Stalin forced the Czechoslovak government to refuse Marshall Plan aid offered by America. In the fall of the same year, the Communists mailed bombs to three non-Communist ministers, one of whom was Drtina. Their inept plan was probably intended to accuse the democrats of mailing them to themselves and thereby provoke a crisis which would culminate in a Communist coup d'état.

The plan didn't succeed. A man from Krajina's electoral district reported to him that the maker of the bombs was a local Communist carpenter. The man was arrested and would have been tried had not the total Communist takeover of Czechoslovakia intervened.

Somewhat naïvely, the democrats hoped that the elections scheduled for May 1948 would fix things. There was every indication the Communists would be nowhere as successful as two years earlier. The trouble was that the Communists knew this as well. They had no illusions about it: the Communists' own poll indicated a rapid fall in popularity, and they had no intention of entrusting their fate to the ballot box.

Their big chance came with the crisis of February 1948. The Communist-controlled Ministry of the Interior had refused to obey a cabinet order to re-instate eight non-Communist police chiefs it had fired. The minister of interior absented himself from the cabinet meetings, claiming illness. With the Communists in open rebellion and the government thus ceasing to function, the democratic ministers had no alternative but to submit their resignation.

But not all of them did. The foreign minister, Jan Masaryk, the son of the first president, did not, and neither did the Social Democrats. The entire democratic strategy rested on the shoulders of the aged and gravely ill President Beneš, who had promised he would not accept the resignations. Sensing that something was afoot, Krajina arrived at the Presidential Castle to remind the president of his promise. He was not received. Krajina left a copy of the Czech National Socialist Party's stand on the crisis at the Castle. In return the president sent word advising Krajina to leave the country. The next day he accepted the resignations, and the new Communist government took office.

On that same day, Krajina met with Drtina to start making plans for leaving the country. But it was not soon enough. The following day Krajina's world was turned upside down when he was gruffly confronted by the police outside of his apartment building. He protested, of course, asserting that he had parliamentary immunity. One of the policemen explained the situation to him — "But you see it's a peaceful revolution" — in Russian.

To his great surprise, he was once more taken to the Peček Palace, formerly the Gestapo headquarters now occupied by the Czech (and of course Russian) police. His interrogator soon explained that he was now in the hands of the new rulers of Czechoslovakia. That didn't mean they would necessarily execute him right away — there was plenty of time for that — but it would depend on whether he agreed to be a spy for the Communists, quite likely in the United States.

Of course, his wife and children would remain behind as hostages, but the quality of their life would depend on how valuable the information he sent back was. "We know you've been successful in spying for Beneš, now you'll have to be equally successful for us. That is, if you want to live!" was the conclusion of their explanation. When Krajina refused to discuss it further they put him into the so-called bunker, the darkened cell where you couldn't stand up, well-known to everyone who had been to the Peček Palace during the Gestapo days. Just before they threw him into the dark hole, Krajina commented to them, "You should be grateful to the Nazis. Thanks to them, all these wonderful innovations are available to you."

He wasn't in his cell long. Marie, who had witnessed his street arrest from her window, promptly entrusted the care of Vladimir junior to her mother and set out to the parliament building and then to the Presidential Castle, where she was told the president couldn't receive her because he was ill. But the office chief, Smutný, listened to her tale of woe and promised to do all he could.

Then Marie visited or called every known prison around Prague, only to be told again and again that her husband was not there. Not in her wildest dreams would she have imagined that the notorious Peček Palace was still in use. A nearby butcher who was also a friend spotted her crying on the street. Filling her shopping bag with delicacies, he accompanied her home.

Late that afternoon the door to Krajina's bunker opened and his interrogator, now less cocky and far less sure of himself, told him that he was being released because a mistake had been made. Marie's intervention with the defeated president had worked.

"At home I was welcomed with open arms but also with strong advice to disappear," remembered Krajina. Knowing that he couldn't take Marie, his daughter, and his two-month-old son with him, the wartime Krajina was instantly back: once more he arranged to spend time away from his home. Soon he was on a train to the border, his anonymity being helped by the general chaos which still reigned following the abrupt Communist takeover.

On February 29, 1948, Krajina's mentor and Minister of Justice Prokop Drtina unsuccessfully tried to commit suicide by jumping from the balcony of his Prague apartment. Gravely injured, he was taken to hospital, and a few days later placed under arrest by the Communists. He remained in prison for the next twelve years.

On the same day at a town called Klatovy in western Czechoslovakia, Krajina was met by a man who took him to the border town of Železná Ruda. There Krajina, while mingling with the skiing crowd, had a relatively leisurely lunch in a restaurant, put on his skis and took the shortest route down to the Bayrische Eisenstein, within the American occupation zone. He was heading for a building flying an American flag. Recognizing his importance, the Americans immediately loaded him into a car to deliver him to Frankfurt. It was there that the prominent Czechs and Slovaks were being concentrated.

A new phase of his life was about to begin.

9
Political Refugee

EARLY IN MARCH of 1948 Vladimír Krajina arrived at the U.S. Army's Alaska House in Oberursel on the outskirts of Frankfurt in the American Occupation Zone of Germany. Shortly afterwards he was elected "sheriff" of Alaska House, in other words, the spokesman for about fifty Czechs interned there whose brains the U.S. Army Intelligence Corps wanted to pick. As an English-speaking hero of the Resistance, Krajina was the logical choice, although it was only a matter of time before he would be leaving for London where, as it seemed at the time, the new anti-Communist Resistance would be taking shape.

In Czechoslovakia there was plenty to be concerned about. There was the attempted suicide of the former Justice Minister Prokop Drtina and the successful one of the first president's son Jan Masaryk, although to this day it isn't clear whether the latter wasn't really a murder. Refugees were beginning to swarm into the American Zone across the border, some eventually arriving by hijacked airplanes. During those Stalinist times such hijackings were considered acts of heroism rather than the crime they became later.

While Krajina was at Alaska House, the American Army asked him to organize intelligence contact with Czechoslovakia. He consulted with other guests at the place — among them was my father (we had recently skied to freedom across the border into Germany, following Krajina's route across the mountains) and a Czech National Socialist journalist named Herben — and asked if they would work with him. While they promised to think about it, both of their wives were strongly opposed. Hadn't their families been through enough already?

In the middle of April, Krajina left Alaska House, supposedly for London, although he didn't arrive there until the middle of the following month. For some reason the American military intelligence wanted to have him isolated, at least temporarily. After he finally arrived in London, Krajina helped with the Czechoslovak Refugee Fund and was occasionally consulted on Czechoslovak matters by the British Foreign Office. He also worried constantly about his family still in Prague. Although contact was maintained with Prague by various means, this was purely for informational purposes; there was no thought yet of organizing anything like a true Resistance movement.

Meanwhile in Prague, within twenty-four hours of Krajina's departure, the police arrived to search his apartment. For quite a few days afterwards, visitors to the place were questioned and Marie was followed wherever she went.

Unknown women and men began arriving at Marie's doorstep with offers to arrange her escape. Marie kept steadfastly refusing these offers, saying there were her children to be considered. Sometimes she would also tell them her husband had left her — supposedly without a word of goodbye — so why should she want to follow him? This was the same "explanation" she had used with the preceding totalitarian regime.

Marie soon sensed that one of the policemen guarding her was not an ardent Communist. One day she asked if he knew what had happened to her husband. He seemed surprised by the question, telling her that Krajina was in England — didn't she listen to the radio?

For the Communists, the spring of 1948 was a time for consolidation.

Although the government was now fully in their hands, there were still too many loose ends that needed tying up. For example, the ailing President Beneš remained in his position and had to be watched constantly, especially in regards to visitors. That situation lasted until June of that year when he refused to sign the new constitution, and resigned instead. The previous month an election had been held according to new rules. A single list of Communist Party-sponsored candidates received 87 percent of the vote. This was something of a surprise because Communist-controlled elections usually resulted in the ninety percentile range.

A world-wide congress of the Czech gymnastic organization, Sokol, was held in Prague that summer, and it resulted in anti-government demonstrations. Further anti-Communist demonstrations took place in September when Beneš died. Any pretext for treating the opposition with kid gloves was now gone: late in the summer of 1948 the law creating Communist concentration camps for dissenters was passed.

That summer, Marie, now well-versed in conspiratorial methods used against totalitarian regimes, was biding her time. Kind people called frequently, offering all sorts of help, and Marie thanked them profusely. Offers to smuggle her abroad still came from different sources almost every week, but Marie didn't trust them. The first credible one came with an offer to outfit a special airplane in which she and her children could leave. It was tempting, but there was no place for her mother, and in the end she refused.

The people she could trust implicitly were her friends from the concentration camp — to whom she referred as the Ravensbrück girls. Their wartime survival largely depended on such trust. In time, one of them handed her half of a postcard while Marie was pushing a baby carriage through a nearby park and told her to trust whoever brought her the other half. Marie hid it under a rug where her daughter eventually found it and nearly threw it away, with Marie salvaging it only at the last moment. She had told no one what it was for.

After a short time, a man brought the other half and told her that the family should be ready soon, taking along only a few absolute necessities. Everything else was to be left at home. The next day her mother went shopping in one direction while she, her daughter and the baby went off in another. Ironically — and perhaps even a bit symbolically — the meeting place for all four of them was in front of the Pankrác prison, where not too long ago Marie had been incarcerated by the Germans. Two cars awaited them there, one filled with armed men who were formerly policemen. Marie handed over the empty baby carriage to her friends, and they headed south, toward Austria.

The fearless servant girl Lojzička, who five years earlier had smuggled out Krajina's message for London from the Gestapo building about the Germans attempting to establish contact with the exile government, helped again. She remained behind in the empty Krajina apartment, occasionally walking across it with loud thumps so that the Communist police in the building would think Marie was still inside.

Near the border, the cars stopped in the middle of woods. They were surprised by a passing red car, which stopped. There was much consternation when Marie heard her name called. It turned out to be a dentist who remembered her from some pre-war function and who invited them to his cottage nearby for some coffee. He must have recognized this as an escape attempt but never mentioned it. Later, Marie became certain that the whole thing had been pre-arranged, that the dentist had been a cog in the elaborate escape machinery.

Then the plan became more complex. They were now accompanied by only one man. The route included a train journey and then a ride on a truck. They were put up at a smugglers' hut, given some potatoes with milk, and provided with a bed. At midnight they set out across a swamp with Marie giving little Vladimir a sedative. Just before they reached the border he woke up and began to cry.

A bottle of milk did the trick. The boy was heavy, and the three-and-a-half-hour walk for Marie seemed like an eternity, especially since she had made the mistake of taking off her stockings. Her shoes became soggy and bruised her feet. But by morning they were in Austria.

Not necessarily safe though. In Prague Marie had been instructed to go to British-occupied Linz, but now was told it was too dangerous. The road to Linz led through the Soviet occupation zone, and the Russians had recently arrested several refugees on it. They boarded a train going to Vienna instead, and there they were put up by an acquaintance.

At an official currency exchange, Marie was unable to exchange the ten dollars she had brought with her because she had no personal documents. At a particularly low point of her stay, she begged at the back door of a restaurant, offering the owner her ten dollars for something to eat. Although he didn't accept her money, she was given half a loaf of bread. Eventually she did manage to exchange the dollars illegally, and now had the Austrian money for the streetcar fare to the British Embassy.

Marie later recalled: "I was surprised how well my situation was understood by the officials of the embassy. They told me they knew the name Krajina and that they would notify my husband in London."

They did. A few days later Marie and her children arrived at a London airport, although her mother had to wait awhile longer. They were met by the much relieved Vladimir senior, who proudly took them to an apartment at Queensgate Terrace he had managed to rent. It was a happy reunion, and for a time they could enjoy London together as a family. Curiously enough, it turned out that they were boarding with a Hungarian countess.

✍

The high point of Krajina's stay in England was his visit to Chartwell, Winston Churchill's home in Kent. The great wartime leader had asked to meet him earlier, right after the war, but then Krajina had been too much engaged in the life and death struggle of the Czech democracy. Now the exiled Krajina was finally to be introduced to Churchill. Both were out of power, although Churchill was destined to become prime minister again in 1951.

Champagne flowed. Giant cigars were lit to help better recall the days full of glory as well as tragedy. Churchill's wife Clementine was there, too, smiling and asking Krajina to identify some of the plants in her garden. Churchill was charm itself, and while he proudly displayed his paintings (which Krajina frankly didn't think much of, but remained silent), he kept returning to wartime events again and again.

The subject of the Nazi super spy Thümmel fascinated Churchill.

Prime Minister Winston Churchill, 1941.

He recalled the Czech Resistance reports from him about Hitler's abandonment of his English invasion plans, about the location of German rocket bases and Hitler's intention to turn south before turning east and thereby postponing the date of Operation Barbarossa to invade Russia. Churchill mentioned that some historians believe that this mistake might have been the key to Hitler's defeat.

Churchill was surprised to hear that Krajina and Thümmel had never met, and that no one else but Krajina was allowed to encode Thümmel's messages. He was impressed by the efficiency with which messages from this highly placed Nazi were handled, and commented that without the information obtained from Thümmel via the Czechs, the war would have been much more difficult to win.

Churchill was sorry to hear Krajina was unable to explain how Thümmel was uncovered by the Nazis. He surmised that if he was able to obtain the highly confidential reports from Hitler's staff, Thümmel must have become a double agent, at least towards the end of the war. With this, Krajina pretty much agreed; to his mind there was no other plausible explanation for Thümmel's betrayal of Captain Morávek, the contact man between the Resistance and Thümmel. Krajina could tell Churchill only that Thümmel was probably executed by the same Gestapo man — Leimer — who had arrested Krajina and who, at the end of the war, in turn had been arrested by him. Later Krajina noted that his visit with Churchill was his highest war decoration.

During Krajina's visit at Chartwell he was taken around the gardens where he noticed a majestic *Pinus ponderosa* from British Columbia. He told Churchill that he would soon be going to Vancouver to lecture at the university there.

British Columbia was the logical choice for Krajina. He had never seen botany and the other natural sciences in the same light as had many scientists of the previous century. Although he had a phenomenal memory and could readily identify plants and trees by their Latin names, he did not see them in isolation, but always together with the ecological system that was conducive to their growth. It followed that he hated to see such a system disturbed: in a film made by the National Film Board of Canada he laments the destruction of a certain high ground in Hawaii where sheep were allowed to over-graze and denude the landscape, not only of the grass but ultimately also of the trees that depended on it.

In that sense, British Columbia with its sparse population mostly concentrated on the Lower Mainland would be an ideal place for him.

The rest of the province had been pretty much left in its pristine condition. Except, of course, for the ruthless clear-cut logging followed by slash burning that was destroying more and more of the landscape as time went on. There was also an abundance of mountainous terrain of the kind that he had adored ever since he had studied the flora of the High Tatras as a young man and around Haleakala Crater a few years later while on a trip around the world.

In the late 1940s, western Canada still had an adventurous ring to it, mostly because so few people had visited and even heard of that part of the world. During the recent Pacific War, names like Guadalcanal, Hong Kong and even Alaska's Aleutian Islands (where the only battle on the American continent was fought), became world-wide concepts. At the time of the Pearl Harbor attack, Vancouver was barely half a century old. Although three times the size of Japan, the entire province of British Columbia had far fewer people than Tokyo. It may have counted among the world's most scenic places, but its importance in world politics, commerce or culture remained fairly limited. Except, of course, for adventurous botanists.

In addition to its fascinating ecological systems, British Columbia held another attraction for Krajina. Vancouver is situated near the 50th parallel — the very same that cuts through Prague's centre at the scenic Old Town Square.

II

THE NEW
WORLD

10

North American
Arrivals

IN THE LATE 1940s Europe was still struggling to repair the enormous war damage, with Britain only slightly better off. Vladimir Krajina and his family had been admitted there as displaced persons and that, somewhat illogically, meant they could not hold a job. During the 1930s Krajina had been an employee of the Kew Gardens administrations, and they would have doubtlessly welcomed him back, but that venue was now closed to him.

It soon became obvious that unlike the World War II effort against the Nazis, the anti-Communist Resistance would not be led from London but from Washington. In the spring of 1949 the American-led Berlin Airlift had succeeded not only in showing Stalin the determination of the West to resist Communist incursions but also in giving birth to the Cold War and NATO. The refugees from Communism, with Vladimir Krajina prominently among them, were longing to resume their normal lives, although Europe as the likely battleground of World War III did not seem a very promising place.

With important scientific experience from around the world coupled with at least rudimentary English, Krajina was luckier than most at this time. He had quickly accepted a two-year appointment as a special lecturer offered by the University of British Columbia in Vancouver. He borrowed money, booked two cabins aboard a Cunard liner, and late in June 1949 the family — wife Marie, her mother, daughter Milena and the infant son Vlad — set out from Southampton to New York.

Except for one day, the crossing was calm. It helped that Krajina had borrowed enough money for second-class tickets instead of the tourist class, which in less elegant times used to be called steerage. Five days later they disembarked in the heat of a New York summer. My father, who himself had arrived at a nearby dock with his family ten short months earlier, noted in his diary on July 1, 1949: "The Krajinas arrived in absolute order."

Father, on the other hand, had arrived without any hint of a job awaiting him, and with the U.S. Immigration official ready to send him to Ellis Island before a wealthy friend intervened. It could therefore be argued that — as opposed to the Krajinas — our arrival was marked by absolute disorder. By the time the Krajinas arrived, however, we were settled in and father was one of those on the dock to welcome the Krajinas.

Already the next morning, five of the leading Czech National Socialists who were in New York met to hear Krajina's report on the London political situation and to discuss the future of their party. The next day Krajina went to Washington to take part in the initial session of the Council for Free Czechoslovakia, and there an oft-repeated anecdote was born. While the Krajinas were still in London, a representative of the Czech-Canadian Bata firm equipped the entire family with new shoes. Used to the European system, Krajina left his pair in front of his hotel room at night to be shined. Apparently the shoes were not as impressive as Krajina thought. The bellboy, who was used to the American system, assumed they were destined for the garbage and helped them on their way.

The next morning, with only socks on his feet, Krajina was desperate. Those were his only shoes. He explained his situation to the man at the front desk, who then personally went across the street to a shoe store to buy him a new pair. But these were too small. As a result, Krajina's memories of his first visit to the U.S. capital were somewhat painful.

Upon returning to New York he visited the Voice of America studios and heard a broadcast in Czech. The same day, there was yet another meeting of the exiled Czech National Socialists. It was agreed that in future their party should move toward the political centre. They were also to strive for closer cooperation with the Social Democrats. This moment has to be seen within the Czechoslovak context: after the war practically all Czech political parties moved further to the left, with one wing of the Social Democrats being almost indistinguishable from the Communists.

Several of those with whom Krajina met in New York voiced their concerns about his planned move to Vancouver. After all, there was his year-and-a-half-old son, his elderly mother-in-law and teenage daughter to consider. They were going to British Columbia, a largely unknown territory supposedly filled with deep woods, grizzlies and, in some minds, even hostile Indians. New York may have been overpopulated, somewhat dirty, hot and humid, but at least it had streets filled with Europeans who had survived there for decades. Who knows what life would be like in Vancouver?

On July 12th the Krajinas left for Montreal. Father noted in his diary that in "the main hall of Grand Central Station once more this group of dispersed democrats gathered to say goodbye." It had been only a bit more than a year since the Communists had staged the Czech takeover, and optimism about a speedy return of democracy still ran fairly high among these Czech politicians. The exile during World War I lasted a little over four years; during the next war it had been six years. Who would have thought that this time it would last forty-one years? Most of those who came to Grand Central Station that day would not live to see the end of the Communist era. Marie had other worries. "This is probably the end of our contact with civilization," she murmured as the train began to move northward.

At Lacolle on the Canadian border their immigration papers were properly stamped and, after a few days in Montreal, the Krajinas boarded another train to Ottawa, from where they would traverse the continent. There they met Ota Hora, a good friend of Krajina and former member of the Czechoslovak parliament — naturally for the Czech National Socialist party.

In the U.S. most of Krajina's political friends were either receiving pensions from the American government or were working in jobs which were fairly equivalent to those they had left behind. For example, the journalist Herben was now the chief editor of the Czech daily *New-yorské listy*, and several others had jobs with the Radio Free Europe, which would begin broadcasting to Czechoslovakia the following year. The situation north of the border in Canada was, however, wholly different.

At this time, immigrants to Canada who were single had to spend their initial year as something like indentured servants, and there was practically no government help of any kind. Hora, who would later attend night school and become a certified public accountant, was employed as a butler, while his wife served as a cook in the household of a high government official. This same high government official took a day off to show the Krajinas the sights of the Canadian capital.

On the other hand, as if to emphasize the dangers of this new land, the Hora's son was in bed with a bad case of poison ivy. Krajina, of course, was familiar with the phenomenon, but his daughter Milena, who was fourteen at the time, remembers that it made her quite apprehensive as to the perilous nature of this new land.

Late that night they boarded another sleek train, in which the Krajinas had booked two compartments. There was a panorama car attached. When they awoke the next morning they were enchanted with the first dark lake of northern Ontario, which appeared complete with a fairy-tale-like small island containing a copse of birch trees. Unfortunately this was a scene repeated hundreds of times. Even the most charming fairy tale loses much of its magic when told several times during the same day.

It was the same with the endless wheat fields of the prairies. But things improved as they neared the Rockies, and the flora changed noticeably. When they unexpectedly stopped in the middle of nowhere, the excited

Krajina leapt out to begin examining the plants, straying further and further away from the train. The worried Marie then came to the door and frantically called out to him to return.

When the train slowly started to move again, he was still some three hundred metres away. He started to run to catch up while his terrified family thought of what they would do if he were not successful. Some ten minutes later with the train now at full speed, things were looking bad, but then he suddenly appeared in the compartment, having caught the last car of a very long train.

He was welcomed by a barrage of reproaches and humbly apologized for all the anxiety he had caused. Seeing that he had not managed to bring with him any of the plant specimens she had seen him collect, Marie exclaimed: "And all that for nothing!"

"For nothing?" responded the astonished Krajina, reaching inside his shirt and coming up with a veritable bouquet of plant samples. A few hours later the train rounded Mt. Robson, and his daughter Milena remembers she had never seen her father so excited.

After three days aboard the train, everyone in the family very much appreciated the arrival in Vancouver. They were met at the station by a university official and taken to their temporary home at the student dormitory. A few days later they moved to UBC's Acadia Camp, which would be their home for the next six years. The conditions were decidedly primitive, but they were together as a family. They had a home again.

Moreover, it was July 20, 1949, exactly five years to the day of the unsuccessful but serious attempt to assassinate Hitler. Under the headline "In Prague, He'd Be Executed — Underground Leader Arrives," the *Vancouver Province* reported that the Krajinas had reached their destination. Apparently once more "in absolute order," because the newspaper saw him as "a friendly Czech" who had made "world-wide jaunts."

And there was optimism all around: the paper reported that "the Krajinas have been in Canada only a week, but they like our country."

11
Newsmaking in the New Land

FOR VLADIMIR KRAJINA, veteran of a trip around the world, and a former resident of ancient European capitals, some of the ways of the sixty-three-year-old city of Vancouver seemed unusual. It hadn't been too long before his arrival that a local ordinance stated that no more than twenty-five cows could be kept within the city limits.

Earlier that year the police had swooped down on several of the city's night clubs because — horror of horrors! — people were consuming alcohol there. Krajina was not a smoker and only a moderate drinker, but being born in Moravia, where the excellent slivovice and local wines were regarded with uncommon pride, British Columbia's local liquor laws were somewhat incomprehensible. For much of his adult life he had been a resident of Prague, where Czech beer was considered manna from heaven and consumed from half-litre glasses at every corner.

Other members of his family were no less confused. In 1949 the province finally allowed the sale of margarine. To Central Europeans and excellent cooks like Marie and her mother, it must have been hard to believe that someone would want to spread this stuff on bread when butter was available without any ration tickets — especially since margarine was sold in a snow-white state with a yellow pill attached, and this pill had to be kneaded in for the margarine to resemble the colour of the real dairy stuff!

The city had few buildings older than fifty years with a vast majority of them, even downtown, made of wood — which was a relatively rare sight in Europe. Except for the green-roofed third version of the Hotel Vancouver and the Marine Building at the foot of Burrard Street, there were no notable man-made landmarks. Certainly nothing like Buckingham Palace or the striking panorama of the Prague Castle.

But modern accomplishments there were, especially in the field of transportation. Kingsway, according to the newspapers, "a strikingly handsome" new six-lane artery between Vancouver and New Westminster, had just opened, and it was then still possible to board a CPR ferry at the heart of downtown and be delivered to the heart of Victoria some three hours later. That was a convenience which has since disappeared.

The Hope-Princeton highway opened the year the Krajinas arrived, providing a new transportation link between the coast and the interior and, perhaps more importantly for Krajina, an easier access to Manning Park, with all its various flora (and some very large fauna) and splendid scenery.

There were also some curious differences. Vancouver, despite following British leadership on most things (even the newspapers of the time slavishly imitated the English format), saw its role within the North American context and had switched its drivers from left to right as early as 1922. By contrast, the Czechs, after much discussion, were forcibly switched by the invading Nazis only in March 1939. There were no accidents in British Columbia connected with the changeover, while several people were killed during the transition period in the newly created Protectorate.

Canada as a whole was undeniably a dynamic entity, always reaching out and growing. In 1949 the country became part of NATO, Newfoundland joined the Canadian confederation, and CP Air inaugurated direct air service to Australia.

Shortly after the Krajinas' arrival, the biggest earthquake in the province's recorded history occurred, measuring 8.1 on the Richter scale. Its epicentre happened to be on Haida Gwaii, then still known as the Queen Charlotte Islands — the very site where twenty-four years later one of the largest provincial ecological reserves would be established and named after Vladimir J. Krajina.

There were other events that pointed out to the Krajinas how different and prone to natural disasters their new homeland was. The year of their arrival, the Capilano River overflowed, taking with it part of the North Shore's Marine Drive, severing for a few days the only land connection with West Vancouver.

On the city's positive side was the fact that few urban centres in the world could boast a harbour as ideal as Vancouver's, and a ridge of mountains over one thousand metres high was within walking distance from its shores. There were no buildings tall enough to obstruct the Krajinas' view of the dramatic mountains.

No wonder that already a few days after his arrival, Krajina started climbing to their tops. Since it was in the high Tatras that his studies of mountain ecology began, he couldn't resist. Unlike in Czechoslovakia, where reaching the peaks required an overnight train trip, here the North Shore summits could be reached within hours.

The trouble was that without a car Krajina had to depend on buses. Sometimes his enthusiasm atop the North Shore mountains got the better of him, and he came back down much too late to catch any public transport. On such occasions he would arrive back at Acadia Camp on foot early in the morning, greeted by the anxious Marie, who reminded him that he was the father of a teenage girl and infant son, and at present the only breadwinner in the family. An accident somewhere on the North Shore mountains would not have been just a relatively simple matter of missing a transcontinental train.

There was no doubt that, despite his demotion — in Prague he had been the Head of the Division of Plant Ecology of one of the oldest universities in Europe, whereas in Vancouver he was merely a special lecturer at one of the youngest — and despite the rudimentary living conditions at Acadia Camp and his lack of mobility, Krajina was happy in

Vancouver. His daughter Milena was now attending the highly regarded University Hill High School, and his infant son was receiving excellent care by his mother and grandmother.

Perhaps most significantly, there were none of those dark political clouds on the horizon which had so consistently kept forming over his head during the last decade. His unshaken belief in God and in the principle that hard work coupled with his ability would once again result in success had never left him.

⁓

At about this time, an affair unfolded that, according to the local newspapers, made Krajina, an otherwise obscure UBC lecturer, into one of the eight biggest Vancouver newsmakers of 1949. In fact he was linked with the "dashing" Anthony Eden, Eleanor Roosevelt, and the Indian Prime Minister, Jawaharlal Nehru.

The affair had begun earlier in London after the Russian news agency Tass, in its bulletin distributed in Great Britain, had resuscitated the old charges against Krajina of collaborating with the Nazis. What piqued Vancouver's interest was the language used by "the tall, gimlet-eyed Lord Vansittart" when he took it upon himself to repudiate the charges on behalf of Krajina. On November 23 in the British House of Lords, he called the Tass bulletin "a piece of impudence," and delivered a scathing attack in which he called the editors servants of "the savage hermits of the Kremlin." He spoke about the special commission which had examined these charges shortly after the war in Czechoslovakia: "The evidence in Kraina's [sic] favour was so overwhelming that he was triumphantly acquitted on all the thirty-six charges put forward — indeed, more: his conduct was rightly found to have been above reproach and he was awarded the two chief Czech military decorations."

For his own part, Krajina had appealed to the courts in Britain, pointing out that he had been libelled by Tass. They found, however, that since Tass claimed it was part of the Soviet state, it enjoyed diplomatic immunity. As a result they recommended that Krajina appeal their decision to the House of Lords.

Vansittart called this an unintentional mockery: "How does anyone expect an unhappy exile living on the smell of an oil rag, not knowing where the next pound is to come from, to find hundreds and hundreds and hundreds of pounds for trial, after trial, after trial?" Although "living on the smell of an oil rag" was probably not an idiom with which Krajina was familiar, he was grateful to the good lord who had taken up his case.

Time magazine picked up on the alleged idea of immunity, reporting that "Lord Vansittart protested such 'preposterous and unprecedented' extension of immunity at a time when all the countries of the Communist empire treat British and U.S. representatives like stink." There was even more newsworthy stuff in Lord Vansittart's speech. After the lower courts' ruling on immunity, he opined that now "there is nothing to prevent the Soviet government from casting the mantle of immunity over any spy ring in this country."

That was alarming enough, but Lord Vansittart went further, pointing out that the Soviet government "does not like to send bachelors to this country, for fear they would pick up Western girls and find out that the West is not so bad after all. In pursuance of that policy there would be nothing illogical in setting up a brothel in this country and classing its inmates as organs of the Soviet government, with just as good a right as Tass — personally I should consider them the more respectable."

No wonder with such tidbits the Vancouver press found Krajina to be such an interesting newsmaker. In the end, however, the chancellor of the House of Lords, Viscount Jowitt, announced that an interdepartmental committee would be established to study the matter, and with that the case was effectively relegated to history.

As a brilliant example of one-upmanship, late that November in Ottawa, the External Affairs Committee of the House of Commons was told that Simeon Shcherbatykh, the only representative of *Tass* in Canada, certainly did not enjoy diplomatic immunity. A Progressive Conservative Member of Parliament, Gordon Grayson, had referred to the recent case in London which upheld the *Tass* plea for diplomatic immunity. Arnold Heeney, external affairs under-secretary of state said that he had no information on the London case, but that in Canada Shcherbatykh did not enjoy such immunity, "being neither a member of the Soviet Embassy here nor on the diplomatic list, despite the fact he represented an agency of the Soviet state."

It would seem then, according to Heeney's statement, Canada was also in no danger of having common bawdy houses set up here by the perfidious Soviets while enjoying diplomatic immunity. Neither, of course, was Vladimir J. Krajina in danger of being libelled by a hostile foreign power.

12
University Beginnings

ALTHOUGH NONE OF HIS colleagues at the botany department had either his education, background or experience, Krajina was content at the University of British Columbia. Not known for always treading softly and diplomatically, he still became quite friendly with Andrew Hutchinson, the department head. Hutchison was a mercifully laid-back type, mild mannered and thoroughly understanding of the turmoil that had until then constituted Krajina's life.

What is more, Hutchinson was an avid Rotary Club member who introduced Krajina to the organization. Krajina found the Rotarians very much to his liking. He discovered in this new land a whole new world beside the academic one — the world of businessmen, doctors, teachers and clergymen who thought it useful to sit down together once a week to share their opinions and generally get to know each other.

Although his focus was primarily on botany, and soon also forestry, Krajina found time for all this on Tuesdays at noon. He and Marie would

Andrew Hutchinson, Head of Botany, UBC, poring over a map with his newly arrived colleague, Krajina, c. 1950. (COURTESY: UBC ARCHIVES)

take the bus downtown. He would meet with his new friends at the Rotary Club while Marie would browse through the department stores to see what was needed and could be afforded.

Krajina's appointment as a lecturer at UBC, which was initially for only two years, had been sponsored by the Lady Davis Foundation of Montreal, which was dedicated to bringing refugee scientists and scholars to Canada. In Krajina's favour in moving up to a full-time position was the very youth of the university which had been established scarcely a quarter of a century earlier. As a consequence, its botany department offered opportunities few other institutions could.

There were vast tracts of forests and numerous lumber companies operating within the province, but little research in forest ecology had taken place. By comparison, Central Europe's forests had been thoroughly mapped with very few old-growth forests left. The woods there were under tight state control and criss-crossed by well-maintained roads. One of the very few exceptions to this was in the Czech Republic. It was the so-called Boubín Primaeval Forest, a 666-hectare tract of original growth in the Šumava Mountains — the same ones which in 1948 Krajina had to cross to freedom. It is a unique tourist attraction that to this day brings in scores of visitors — something akin to the badlands of Alberta with its Dinosaur Provincial Park.

By contrast, much of British Columbia consisted of old-growth forests. There were few forest roads in those areas, but also ruinous clear-cutting in the coastal areas near large bodies of water. Krajina, always the conservationist and a pioneering ecologist, saw his opportunity here. According to him, more important than the study of individual plants and trees was a consideration of the entire ecological system. Of course, it required a thorough knowledge of the individual plants and trees, but that, due to his encyclopedic mind, was rather taken as a given. Because lumber constituted an important part of the wealth of the province, was it not logical to take stock, not only of what we have, but also how we came to have it?

Krajina realized that practically no research had been done in Canada in bryology, which is the study of mosses, an important component in the understanding of forest ecology. Already one year after his arrival he began to fill this void by writing a paper for the journal *The Bryologist*, entitled "New Species of the Genus Dicranella from British Columbia." The year after that he came out with a paper which clearly indicated the direction he was taking. It was called "The Significance of Bryophytes and Lichens for the Characterization of Some Forest Associations on Vancouver Island."

With the publication of such papers, Krajina's appointment at the university was soon regularized. In 1951 he was appointed assistant professor, two years later, associate professor and also member of the Faculty of Forestry. And ten years after his arrival in Canada he was promoted to full professor, as he had been in post-war Czechoslovakia.

In 1952 he wrote an interim report about his study of the "Ecological Classification of the Forests of the Eastern Part of Vancouver Island." Now there could be no doubt as to which botanical road he was taking.

Krajina (left) with W. Van Heek and another forester,
viewing logging operations in the Kalum area, north
of Terrace. (PHOTO: K. KLINKA)

✍

Those were busy years, not only for his academic life but for his personal one. The first decade is an extremely important period of acclimatization for every immigrant. During that time the past usually begins to recede slowly into memory, with history playing an important role. It is either a place to visit in order to evoke heart-warming memories or to studiously avoid to keep out nightmares.

The present, on the other hand, is no longer a constant challenge in the new environment, but eventually becomes an everyday affair — in the good sense of the expression — losing many of the unreasonable expectations with which it tends to be encrusted. In other words, the immigrant is gradually forced to come face to face with reality. A purely economic immigrant often finds his new situation in a foreign land full of strange customs, which are on occasion difficult to cope with; at times doubts may even set in as to whether he had made the right decision in leaving his homeland.

With true political refugees this is the case less frequently. Because the past has been fraught with danger, they are forced to burn some bridges. Such was certainly the case with Krajina: he knew that the past had been life-threatening too many times, while now he had found safety for his family. Moreover, he also had his beloved flowers to study. No trade had to be learned or new discipline studied; all that was needed was the proper adjustment to his new surroundings.

According to sociologists it took about a decade for most post-war displaced persons in the New World, at least those of the middle class, to once again reach the economic level they had earlier enjoyed in Europe. Krajina rose substantially toward this level with the purchase of a car in 1951. But there was a catch: prior to his acquisition of this shiny used Oldsmobile, he had never driven an automobile, much less owned one. Before the war he was too poor, during the war there were obvious reasons, and afterwards as the general secretary of a powerful political party, he rated a car with a chauffeur. Consequently, according to some, with his absent-minded driving habits he became something of a menace on the road.

In fact, even many years after buying the car, Krajina's driving skills had still not improved. A case in point occurred when he and Marie were taking the newly arrived immigrants, Věra Roller and her son, around Vancouver. Věra Roller recalls the incident: "We were coming down some hill, in front of us the sun was setting, and suddenly there was a crash. Vladimir had run into another car. My son whispered to me: 'Isn't this a bad omen of sorts?'"

It really wasn't. The son has since done very well in the business world of North America, and although there have been many more near misses, everyone in the Krajina family has survived them with no ill effects. Just like the Gestapo and the Communists, the car was no match for Krajina who, after all, had always specialized in narrow escapes.

Milena at her graduation from UBC with her proud father. (Krajina's hat and robe were home-made, copying a model worn by the 15th-century Czech martyr, Master Jan Hus, rector of Charles University.)

The Krajinas definitely rose to middle class status during the mid-1950s with the purchase of a house on Chancellor Boulevard in the prestigious university district. Vladimir junior was now in grade school and daughter Milena about to graduate from the university at her doorstep. While the children's English was impeccable, Czech was spoken at home and both she and her brother remain fluent to this day.

Already at Acadia Camp and then later in the house on Chancellor Boulevard, the growing number of Czech students studying at the university had discovered that on Saturday afternoon Marie's mother baked tasty Czech *buchty* pastry and they made sure that their visits were timely — after lunch on Saturday. Soon, regular Czech-style dinners evolved from the occasion, with sometimes as many as ten people crowding around the table. A somewhat more lasting result was that daughter Milena married one of the visitors, Slavomir Janda, who eventually became a high official in the Canadian Ministry of Finance.

There were other natives of Czechoslovakia with whom Krajina became friends in British Columbia. Among them were the mighty Koerner brothers, who came from Nový Hrozenkov in Moravia. There were four of them — Leon, Otto, Walter and Theodor — and they truly revolutionized the provincial lumber industry.

The Krajina family in front of their house at
4960 Chancellor Boulevard, 1957.

The origins of the Koerners' business had a somewhat unusual beginning. While on a trip to California, Leon and his wife Thea stopped in Vancouver, where Thea contracted mumps. Since the family had been lumbermen in Central Europe, her husband used the time while she was recuperating to check out the local lumber industry in British Columbia. He found conditions highly favourable and invited his brothers to join him. His stroke of genius was to rename western hemlock — which was thought to be "uncuttable and unsaleable" — under the more acceptable name of Alaska pine. He figured out how to cut it and kiln-dry it efficiently, and then introduced new uses for it. The lumber-hungry World War II did the rest to make them all millionaires several times over.

When Krajina made their acquaintance, the Koerners were already exceptionally wealthy. In 1955, as a token of gratitude for being allowed "to start their life over again in a free and democratic country," the oldest brother and his wife endowed the Leon and Thea Foundation with its first million. It was the third private foundation in the province, and the first to be founded by immigrants. Through the Koerners' immensely successful Alaska Pine Company, the Czech immigrant community had acquired a credibility among the business and cultural community, and through the Leon and Thea Foundation this credibility spilled over into the cultural community. It wouldn't be long before Krajina's achievements would do the same in the scientific one.

There was also the Náloš family who, along with another Czech native, the 17th-century Prince Rupert, have the distinction of having a place in British Columbia named after them. It's Nalos Landing, a one-time location of a family sawmill which, alas, no longer exists.

Krajina's contacts with the Koerners and executives of other lumber companies meant that he was almost always able to find much needed employment for Czech students in the forests. This was somewhat curious, because already during this early period he was offering harsh critiques of their sometimes ruthless logging practices.

The Krajinas have always been a family filled with compassion. Born a Catholic, Krajina had been greatly helped during his two years in hiding by the Czech Brethren, a Protestant sect who are known in North America as the Moravian Brethren. In Vancouver the Krajinas discovered the United Church on the university grounds, where they were warmly received, with Marie active in the ladies' groups and Krajina soon becoming an elder. During the 1950s, hearing about the suffering in Czechoslovakia, the congregation offered to help through donations of clothes, eventually even postage.

The Krajinas now straddled several fairly disparate groups. Vladimir was a member of academe and the Rotary Club; both of them were active among the Czechoslovaks and in the United Church. In all these activities and memberships they constituted something of a classic immigrant family, as government booklets of the time liked to describe the newcomers.

Because of the earlier incident with the House of Lords, Krajina was frequently consulted by the Vancouver press on matters involving European Communism. He was not, however, consulted on one matter which was close to his heart, because in far-away Vancouver the affair seemed to lack the immediacy with which it was viewed in Europe. In May 1950 in Prague the trial of Milada Horáková began.

Dr. Horáková's personal history was filled with dark times. A Prague lawyer, she had been arrested during the war for her Resistance activity. After a trial in Dresden, where the Nazi prosecutor proposed a death sentence, she successfully defended herself in flawless German, and her sentence was reduced to eight years in prison. She was serving her sentence in Bavaria when the war ended. Like Marie, it was her deep faith in God that had helped her through the five years of harsh imprisonment, which had been preceded by torture at the hands of the Gestapo.

After the war she was elected to the Czechoslovak parliament as a Czech National Socialist deputy. It was here that Vladimir came to know her and admire her unshakeable faith in democracy buttressed by basic human decency.

While her husband managed to escape moments before the Communists came to arrest him, Milada Horáková wasn't as lucky. The Communist regime needed a conspiracy to justify its harsh measures, and in May 1950 a carefully programmed show trial with Horáková began in Prague. On May 27, despite pleas for clemency from, among others, Winston Churchill and Eleanor Roosevelt, Milada Horáková was hanged.

Few had been as shaken by this monstrous trial and its conclusion as much as Krajina. Horáková's wartime and post-war history had been too close to his own, and it further convinced him he had been right to escape without his family immediately after the Communist takeover.

More controversial was the trial of Rudolf Slánský, which came later that year. Slánský had been the general secretary of the Czechoslovak Communist Party, holding the same position that Krajina held four years before with the Czech National Socialists. But here the similarity ended. Until his arrest, Slánský had had been an ardent Stalinist, serving as the Soviet dictator's willing and enthusiastic accomplice in his many crimes, even murders.

This time the Vancouver press paid more attention when Slánský and a group, largely composed of Jewish members of the Communist Party, were accused of being "Trotskyite-Titoists," who were planning to overthrow the regime. Ten of them were sentenced to death and executed before the end of the year.

In Vancouver Krajina told the *Province* newspaper that he knew the charges were bogus, saying that "all these men are the same breed I have been fighting for years." Nevertheless, he added, if the world had fewer of them, he would be the last to complain. At the time, Krajina saw the executions as being the result of a personal conflict between the Czechoslovak President Klement Gottwald and Rudolf Slánský. It has since been established that the judicial murder of Slánský and his colleagues was not the result of a struggle between Gottwald and Slánský, but the result of a direct order from Stalin. In fact, Slánský and Gottwald had been great friends while in a Moscow exile during the war as well as in post-war Czechoslovakia. But as Czechoslovak president, Gottwald lived in perennial fear of the murderous generalissimo, and would never dream of disobeying him, Slánský had to go.

There was a good reason for Krajina's miscalculation: it was incomprehensible to him that someone could commit murder either out of fear, ideology or loyalty. It was the biologist in him, in conjunction with his Christianity and humanism, which dictated this high respect for all life.

In 1956 the attention among the Soviet satellites shifted to Hungary, with the brutal Soviet re-occupation of the country. Krajina, now a year-old citizen of Canada, naturally condemned the Russian invasion and welcomed the subsequent influx of Hungarian refugees into Canada. Unique among them was the arrival of fourteen faculty members and some two hundred students from Hungary's Sopron University who, after a period of "conditioning" in Powell River, began their academic year as students at the Sopron University division of the University of B.C.'s Department of Forestry in September 1957.

Unlike previous refugees from Central Europe, some of the Hungarians resented having classes scheduled in old army huts and having to live in relatively primitive conditions. Several even started grumbling that perhaps, since there had been invitations from other countries, it had been a mistake to come to Canada. Eventually the primary problem of the language barrier was whittled down and relations improved, although none of the students or faculty reached the erudition or prominence of Krajina.

In 2007, Professor Antal Kozak of the Department of Forest Resources Management summed up the experience of the Sopron in British Columbia: "If we examine the changes that occurred in B.C. forestry practices between the early '60s up until now, we notice a significant change for the better. No, there is no scientific proof that two hundred or so Hungarian foresters played an important role in these changes, but we would like to believe that they did." By 1961 the last of the Sopron students graduated and the institution was merged with the UBC Forestry Faculty. Four of the Hungarian instructors became members of that faculty and thereby Krajina's colleagues.

13

The Weyerhaeuser
Connection

IN THE SUMMER OF 1954 Krajina received an invitation to assess the effectiveness of Weyerhaeuser's forestry practices by visiting the company's tree farms. Later that year he produced his report, *Some Ecological Observations on Weyerhaeuser Tree Farms*, which is probably the most succinct statement Krajina ever made about his ecological philosophy.

Although no longer what it once was, Weyerhaeuser today still remains a giant among forest companies. It also has a colourful history, even quotable principles. For example, already at the start of the last century its founder felt that "the way to make money is to let the other fellow make some too." It doesn't quite measure up to the Golden Rule but at a time when industrial robber barons ruled, it would do.

Moreover, during the 1930s, at a time when kidnapping gained prominence in the U.S. with the Lindbergh case, the grandson of the company's founder was abducted. There was a happy ending, though, as both he and the ransom money were recovered, and the kidnappers apprehended. And for a grand finale, the young man eventually became the company's president.

Weyerhaeuser was also progressive in its methods. Concentrating mainly on producing lumber, Weyerhaeuser would have probably gone under during the Depression were it not for its radical diversification in beginning to produce pulp, which saved it from bankruptcy. Then, with the war just around the corner, it diversified further by going into the production of plywood and panelling. In 1940 it established its first tree farm, a move helped by the Pacific Northwest states setting lower taxes for timberland, thereby promoting reforestation. By and large it could be said that Weyerhaeuser had been paying attention, not only to market demands but its future requirements as well.

Considering Krajina's recent struggles with Germany, it might be thought ironic that he was now writing a report for a firm that had been founded at the turn of the century by a German immigrant. But perhaps not as ironic as it would seem at first sight. The early and often brilliant biological treatises Krajina wrote were in the scientific language of the time, namely German.

It is unclear how Krajina, at this time a newly minted assistant professor at UBC, came to the attention of Weyerhaeuser. Perhaps his German articles or some of the later ones in English caused the company to take notice.

The Weyerhaeuser report is uncharacteristically diplomatic for Krajina. He goes out of his way to record how impressed he was by Weyerhaeuser's "advanced forestry department with an able staff of foresters." But he quickly follows it by stating that "to the extent that foresters do not control the cutting and logging operations in the virgin stands . . . they cannot be blamed for certain reforestation failures" — which appears to be a scarcely veiled shot at management.

Before one could wink, Krajina returns to praising the forest caesars instead of burying or even blaming them: "The author found excellent cooperation by the foresters, not only among themselves in the Company, but with the foresters of different other companies [sic] and the State Forest Service. Only from such cooperation, between all foresters and forest scientists, can it be expected that progress in a sustained yield forest policy will be attained." Somewhere amongst all that tortured syntax and those irrelevant adjectives there is a message of praise, although once more it is limited to field personnel. Krajina was clearly more at home alongside foresters than their managers in air-conditioned offices.

One of the main thrusts of Krajina's Weyerhaeuser report lies in his explanation of the close interrelationship between organisms and environment. Since ecology is concerned with both, his studies must concern themselves with plants as well as animals. Then he goes on to say "what every forester knows": that two trees of the same species may reach a different size, depending on which habitat they are growing in. Based on that observation, he points out that it is the aim of ecology to study the habitat conditions and the growth rate of trees. At the same time he warns that such conditions are "much more complicated than they seem to be at first glance."

Krajina goes on to say that while some people think that a forest can be defined as a stand of trees, either of the same or several different species, this definition is incomplete. A true ecologist sees the whole picture: a composite of plants and animals which had also developed within a complex of local climate and soil.

According to him, an ecology-conscious forester must obtain a basis on which to decide whether second-growth forests should be subject to regeneration, either by limited or complete planting. "Every forester should be proud to know that he may establish forest stands better than those yielded by nature," Krajina concludes.

His very next paragraph establishes a caveat which should probably be put on his commemorative plaque on the façade of UBC's Department of Botany and/or Forestry Department, should such a plaque ever be contemplated: "Forest resources are natural resources which should not be exploited by the methods used in mining, where the products cannot be regenerated. Forest resources should be kept for a sustained yield through all generations."

Towards the end of his introduction to the Weyerhaeuser Report Krajina warns that forests in virgin conditions are rapidly disappearing and often only small portions now remain. In an early reference to his subsequent triumph scored with ecological reserves, he advises that a representative portion of them "should be saved intact for future study."

In his introduction Krajina comes up with the following parable: "The man who is sick and in need of medical attention needs a physician who can see his difficulty as a whole and is able to investigate his body. It would be probably insufficient for the physician's decision if he did not have an opportunity to see and interrogate the patient, but instead obtained a list of meals the patient usually eats and the conditions of his home (i.e. environmental factors). The ecologist is in a similar situation when he is asked to provide the basis for forestry practices and cannot see trees anymore because they were cut and logged." He then concludes this section by explaining that the report is meant only to stimulate foresters to make their own observations.

In the next section he lists the various trees and the general ecology, (including a treatise on the ponderosa pine forests in the Klamath Falls Area by T.C. Brayshaw), and goes on to identify plants and animals that inhabit the area.

Krajina, with his trademark ice-axe, which he used as a walking stick, with Forest Service inventory personnel at Bell Irving River. (PHOTO: K. KLINKA)

The most contentious part of Krajina's report is saved for last. Here he condemns logging with the help of a caterpillar tractor (a common practice at the time), because it was extremely damaging to the soil. The soil is heavily compacted, with aeration greatly reduced, the bulldozer blade disrupting soil stratification. Somewhat surprisingly, Krajina then suggests that horses should be used instead, which may have been a realistic option sixty years ago. But he is not unequivocally against the use of bulldozers, rather suggesting that such machinery should be used more judiciously. On one Weyerhaeuser tree farm he allows that caterpillar tractors have eliminated "vigorously growing shrubs."

There are other bits of advice in the report which suggest the need for greater expenditures on the part of the forest company. For example, he advises initially the overstocking of newly reseeded areas, but then warns that such areas must be thinned and pruned at least twice to reduce the presence of insects and pathogens.

As far as harvesting is concerned, Krajina writes that it is "of most immediate importance" that methods whereby only commercially useful trees are cut and those of lesser value left standing be soundly rejected. He also lists the order in which various species should be cut.

That is the gist of Krajina's 1954 suggestions for Weyerhaeuser. His son assumes that he was well paid for them, but more important is the fact they were not thrown into the nearest waste basket. Already in March 1954, Royce O. Cornelius, assistant managing forester at Weyerhaeuser, used Krajina's comments in his "Summary from the 1954 Annual Forestry Reports of Information and Recommendation of Interest to the Forestry Research Staff":

> The year was unique in its external stimuli. The first of these was the visit of Dr. Vladimir J. Krajina, who made an ecological study of the area. . . . Dr. Krajina's report provided an added reason for beginning now to examine some of the justifications for a more intensive forest practice. Three projects of the Centralia research center are aimed in this direction: (1) an exploratory study in soils by Steinbrenner; (2) an experiment in thinning directed by Wiksten; (3) an experiment in brush control by aerial spraying directed by Lauterbach. . . .

The purpose of this section is to submit our reactions to some of the proposals made by Dr. Krajina. We agree with his contention that an intensive forestry program should be based on sound ecological principles. We are impressed by the amazing gap between the present practice and that envisioned by a purist. It is gratifying that some of his suggestions have given impetus to experimental work.... We are grateful for the stimulus which has caused us to examine our own program rather critically.

Up to here one would surmise that the Krajina evaluation was a roaring success in every respect. But as usual, there is also the last section which, after heaping praise on the impetus giver, gets down to brass tacks:

In two respects, however, we must report a difference of opinion. First, Dr. Krajina contends that a trained ecologist can evaluate the situation without the support of measurements of effects. That is contrary to our experience....

Second, the report itself is mainly a recitation concerning the presence of certain vegetative communities [sic]. It does not explain their significance....

We recommend the inclusion of ecological factors in our existing studies, especially those that are measurable. We advise against radical departures from our present program until experimental evidence is available which indicates the advisability of such action.

Even to a layman these criticisms seem somewhat unfair in the manner of setting up straw men. Nowhere in Krajina's report does he suggest that an ecologist should dispense with scientific measurement. It is rather quite likely he considered it a given — something that does not need to be even mentioned.

And in view of the fact that his report was already submitted scarcely two months after his observations, it would seem that, besides accuracy, expediency must have figured highly in his mind. By its structure it is clear that the report was not meant as a textbook on ecological interrelationships.

It is apparent, moreover, that during the next few years Krajina's findings reverberated through Weyerhaeuser reports and publications.

The *Weyerhaeuser Magazine* in November 1955 reported that the company has begun experiments aimed at the reduction of the damage by caterpillar tractors, using ideas introduced by Krajina. Specifically the magazine says, "Around landing and loading areas, soils are often severely compacted by logging cats and the weight of logs, making restocking with trees difficult and reducing the rate of growth."

The 1956 activity report of the Weyerhaeuser Forestry Research Center in Centralia, Washington, starts off with the announcement that the year "has been marked by numerous significant adjustments at the Forestry Research Center. We are starting needed research in the essential fields of Physiology, Pathology, and Wildlife Biology." It then lists eight major areas, all of which had been covered in the Krajina report.

The year 1958 was fast approaching when Krajina would be promoted to full professor on the basis of his academic papers. Purely scientific treatises may be just the thing for academic advancement, but to become relevant beyond the walls of the ivory tower something more substantial is required. And that was precisely the role Krajina's Weyerhaeuser report had played.

14

Foundations for
the Reserves

IF THE 1950S WERE used by Krajina to develop his ideas about preserving tracts of provincial land for research, then the 1960s were the time to lay the foundations for such tracts. This was done by delineating and mapping the different biogeoclimatic zones of British Columbia.

The impulse for this work began in 1959 when he stopped in Hawaii for a lecture on his way to a Pacific Science Congress in Tokyo. Two years later an invitation came to return to his beloved islands as a visiting professor at the University of Hawaii. Having studied the ecological systems of the islands during his earlier around-the-world trip, he was now able to compare what had happened there during the intervening four decades. His research around the campus in Hawaii resulted in a twenty-eight-page paper, "Identification and Numbers of Plants Planted on the Campus of the University." He also wrote an analysis, entitled "The Ecosystem Concept in Forestry," which became part of the papers presented at the Fifth World Forestry Congress that year.

A larger project was his paper identifying the islands' twelve biogeo-climatic zones. "The Hawaiian Islands are a fascinating area for study of many biogeocoenoses, floristically either composed of native vegetation or introduced. These islands should become a classic region for the synecological studies in tropical and subtropical climates. Such studies would become a scientific basis for multiple land use in similar regions," he concluded. Translated into everyday English, Krajina claimed that the islands offered the possibility of a study of organic and inorganic components within an ecological community, and he predicted the study would become something of a paradigm for such studies in similar regions.

From there it was just a hop, skip and jump to the idea of recognizing the biogeoclimatic zones of British Columbia. Since the end of the 1950s Krajina and his students had been concentrating on studies of ecological systems such as those of the Columbia River basin. During the early 1960s their studies escalated to the more general ecosystem classification of forests.

In 1964 Krajina convened a symposium on biogeoclimatic zones in Vancouver, and the following year he triumphantly published a research paper, *Biogeocoenosis of British Columbia*. The foundation on which the ecological reserve system could eventually be built was now complete.

Slightly modified over the years, these zones today represent different combinations of soil, physiography, climate and vegetation, and are the basis of much of the provincial forest and land use planning. There are fourteen of them, subdivided into subzones and variants. The five largest are the Alpine tundra; Boreal white and black spruce; Engelmann spruce-subalpine fir; Coastal western hemlock and sub-boreal spruce. Together, they constitute almost three-fourths of the province's area.

Considering some earlier conflicts between Krajina and some of the forest company executives, a booklet describing the various provincial formations and zones is significant. By 1976, when it was published, the praise for the author's methodology and "the aid in selection of species both for planting and subsequent spacing and cleaning of a plantation," is notable since, along with the Van Dusen Gardens, the booklet's co-publisher was the MacMillan Bloedel Company, the province's largest forest firm at the time. Obviously the earlier rift between the sometimes impetuous Krajina and the archaic lumbermen had been at least partially healed.

Much later, in 1985, Mohan K. Wali of the New York College of Environmental Science and Forestry wrote that "the life and times of Vladimir Joseph Krajina coincide with phenomenal advances in the conceptual and empirical development in ecology, and he has been a distinguished contributor to both."

Although Wali several times referred to the "elegance" of Krajina's classification methods, he also indicated that they had not been without detractors. Krajina had been challenged by those who asked why there should be any classification at all, and whether it was possible to classify the unclassifiable. The Braun-Blanquet system of classification published in 1928 was the target of much of their criticism. While plant associations were becoming formalized in Europe, some scientists on this continent expressed doubts about its objectivity and uncertain methodology.

Krajina had modified some of the more rigid aspects of the Braun-Blanquet system, but he was sure that "without classification there is no science of ecosystems, and no ecology. And, indeed, no science." It should be remembered that his phenomenal memory coupled with fourteen-hour workdays placed him, when it came to classification, far ahead of many of his colleagues. Here was also where his strong emphasis on field studies proved crucial.

⁂

An interesting footnote to all this was Krajina's 1964 summer, his first foray into the Arctic. Krajina spent sixty days in the area with his son and two graduate students. He spent it researching the ecology of the Mackenzie River Delta and mapping biogeoclimatic zones. The trip was made possible by a grant from the federal government and UBC's Arctic and Alpine Research Committee. Good use was made of their time in that they returned with more than 1,000 pounds of materials to be examined.

On one score, however, he was less successful, and this was in his economic predictions for the area. An article in the *Vancouver Province* betrayed his lack of training in the field of economics. After his return from the shores of the Mackenzie River, the *Vancouver Province* newspaper ran with the headline: "Most Everything is Perfect for Vegetables Up North." In the article Krajina reported that "the soil up there is quite suitable for the production of vegetable crops." While admitting in passing that the growing season in the delta consisted of only two months, he confidently claimed that the almost continuous daylight compensated for this. In the article he allowed that the high cost of transportation could be a detrimental factor, but also said that the population of the delta "could be increased and made self-sufficient with locally produced crops." This assessment of northern economic possibilities was clearly hopelessly utopian. His remarks to the media would resemble those in his MacMillan Lecture eight years later, where he often strayed into areas where his footing was not at all certain.

But eventually the Arctic had to take a back seat. Early in 1968 Krajina saw a giant stride being made towards his ultimate goal: a committee was formed by the provincial government entrusted to deal with "potential ecological reserves," and this project would now involve much of his energy and vision.

⌁

Before turning to the ecological reserves, a word is in order about the Krajinas' family life. During the 1960s Krajina's son became a teenager. Although Krajina considered this young man something of a post-war miracle baby, it was not the usual father-son relationship which developed. For example, Vlad junior notes that they never played sports together, although the North American emphasis on ball throwing as opposed to the European ball kicking may have played a part in this. There was also the more than usual age difference, plus the fact that the older Krajina, at least according to his son, regarded all sports as somewhat useless. On the other hand, his daughter notes that in his youth Krajina was an expert high jumper, and in his pre-war days in Prague he played tennis. She also notes that his more than usual enthusiasm for the sport may have been caused by the opportunity to make later contacts for his Resistance work.

But there is no doubt that as soon as his son could stand on skis

Krajina started taking him up Mt. Seymour. Initially there was no money for tows so it was cross-country skiing on the meadows only. For the same reason, at lunchtime they would sit in the car with the heater on, eating sandwiches prepared at home by the ever-inventive Marie, who always added a piece of healthful green pepper to the menu.

Krajina may have joined the Rotary Club and he and Marie may have been active in the local United Church, but at home things were essentially done the Czech way. Perhaps this was due to the strong presence of Marie's mother — one of Krajina's greatest admirers. Although Marie's mother spoke fluent Czech, German and Hungarian, she never did learn English. The Czech language and customs remained their main means of communication at home.

There seemed to be always Czech students sleeping on the floor or staying in the basement and, on weekends, according to Vlad junior, "long lunches would deteriorate into long afternoons full of coffee with whipped cream, where father would let his hair down."

All these Czech influences had certain unpleasant consequences. Vlad junior initially lagged behind in English reading at school, and Krajina, who had always excelled in everything, was not happy. Remedial measures had to be taken. "He had incredible cognitive abilities and a chess-like mind," Vlad junior remembers, "and was capable of studying endlessly. The arts and humanities were all right, but in the end only science was truly important." Vlad junior, who is today an avid downhill skier, fly fisherman and one who would never say no to an evening with his buddies, naturally arranged his life somewhat differently. "Father always complained that he didn't have time for friends," he recalls.

This wasn't completely true because some old ones did appear occasionally. Like the baritone and later respected Hollywood actor Jan Rubeš and a distant relative and piano virtuoso, Rudolf Firkušný. Also his friend from the underground, the novelist Zdeněk Němeček, formerly a Czechoslovak ambassador in Denmark and now a writer for Radio Free Europe. One summer evening while vacationing in British Columbia, Němeček, his bald head covered by a stylish black beret, unexpectedly appeared at Krajina's door, holding a cardboard box filled with several layers of beautiful rainbow trout interspersed with fern leaves.

It was that particular visit which perked up Vlad junior's interest in fishing. A few years later he casually asked his father whose picture it was hanging on his office wall. He was informed that it was writer-naturalist and later chancellor of the University of Victoria, Roderick Haig-Brown.

"You've met him?" gasped the now avid fly fisherman Vlad junior, and found out that his father knew him very well indeed, as he was one of the greatest supporters of the ecological reserve idea. But when Vlad junior asked to meet him he was informed that, alas, his hero had died a few weeks before.

And there were local friends as well. Krajina lunched regularly at the university's faculty club and attended evening social affairs there at which he became known as a vigorous if not altogether expert waltz and polka enthusiast.

For Vlad junior at home, there were subtle and not so subtle pressures in the direction of botany. Like all those science books under the tree at Christmas, and outings which would start out as hikes and end up as field trips. On one such trip, he and his father were driving just south of the border, equipped with an old liquor bottle full of cold coffee. The coffee was cold because on previous trips Krajina kept absent-mindedly breaking the thermoses with which he had been supplied — until they became too expensive and he was allotted only bottles. But it was, after all, a research trip and Krajina, who was driving, kept veering off to the left side of the road whenever he saw an interesting plant there. Simultaneously he was also taking an occasional mighty swig on his cold coffee, achieving all that through expert multitasking without taking his foot off the gas pedal.

The feat caught the attention of a state trooper, who was convinced he was seeing a different phenomenon — not just a curious botanist with bad driving habits. It took quite a bit of explanation and an examination of the bottle's contents before Krajina was let off with a warning and advice henceforth to always stay on his side of the road.

On their trips together Krajina remarked to his son that in North

America people they would meet on wilderness paths never spoke to them. He sadly missed the camaraderie he experienced in similar remote places on European paths, particularly Czech and Slovak ones.

Although Vlad junior never learned to burn with equal passion for plants and ecology, he fondly remembers their moments together, with his father's face excited by the infinite variety and beauty of the nature around them. During the early 1970s he recalls walking along Long Beach on Vancouver Island with him when he had a strange premonition this would be the last time. He was right. Then in his twenties, his ambitious studies would quite likely have prevented it. Today he holds degrees in medicine from Dalhousie as well as biochemistry from the University of British Columbia.

There was one exception though, a very short but unusually poignant one during their Czechoslovak trip in 1990. Few moments topped the emotional nostalgia content of a walk with his father through the forest called Hošanka at Krajina's native Slavice. The eighty-five-year-old Krajina, now bent and his gait uncertain, was walking with the added insurance of a sturdy cane. Despite it, there was a sparkle in his eye. He was back, where it all began, where he had first felt the wonder of nature along with the miracle of our existence on this earth. For a moment he was the little boy again whose hair above his temples was so thick and straight that it resembled a small pair of mischievous horns. This was where the fire had been lit. It constituted one of those mystical fleeting moments in life when it all falls into a pattern and makes sense, and Krajina's son felt it too.

Daughter Milena also successfully resisted her father's call to the wild and spent much of her life in theatre and opera. She was flattered when told that her father had named one of his newly found plants after her, although somewhat disappointed when she found out that it was a moss.

⌁

Throughout much of 1968, Krajina, like many Czechs, was filled with hope about the ongoing attempts to liberalize Communist Czechoslovakia, what was called the Prague Spring. All of this ended in August of 1968 when the Soviets invaded Czechoslovakia. At the time Krajina was serving as the president of the Vancouver branch of the Czech and Slovak Association of Canada. This was an organization that had become somewhat dormant during the years before the invasion as its members had become elderly. As the Czechs and Slovaks are notoriously efficient in the art of assimilation, and there was also a dearth of newly arrived immigrants, this development was inevitable. But it was unexpectedly changed after the Soviet invasion by the arrival of some fifteen thousand Czechs and Slovaks, whose admittance into Canada had been negotiated by the organization's head office in the East.

Everyone within the Czechoslovak community was mobilized: furniture and household items were collected, help with job searches was provided along with advice on how best to adjust to the Canadian lifestyle. A fiery orator and now also an esteemed member of the community, Krajina was in great demand as a speaker at gatherings around town.

From that time there is an event in connection with Krajina that the newly arrived Miloš Zach remembers well. But as a preamble to it he tells how in 1948 in Prague he attended a meeting of the Czech National Socialist youth, where the speaker was the party's general secretary, Vladimír Krajina. His wartime exploits were by that time well-known, and as soon as Krajina finished his formal speech, Zach became part of a human wave which enveloped the speaker's podium, asking Krajina all sorts of questions. Sensing all that enthusiasm, the young Zach took courage and asked Krajina how best to resist the Communists who used democratic freedoms to destroy democracy.

"That is precisely the reason why I am addressing you young ones today," Krajina answered. "So that you would become politically active and not stand idly by, watching the Communists usurp power."

Twenty years later they met again in Vancouver. According to Zach, Krajina marched into the room dressed in a suit and a tie, carrying a heavy briefcase. He sat down and went to work. Someone introduced the engineer Zach to Krajina, whose first question was: "So what can I do for you?"

That surprised Zach who was not used to such pragmatism. At that time in Prague people had neither the energy nor desire to help others outside their family circle. Zach told Krajina about their meeting at the rally two decades before in Prague, and while Krajina remembered the rally, he didn't remember Zach personally.

In spite of that, he again became highly practical and asked about Zach's qualifications and experience. He made copious notes in a thick and important looking notebook, from which all sorts of papers and visiting cards protruded, then pronounced his verdict: "There is still plenty of time. Finish this English course you are taking and call me six weeks before it's over. And now will you please excuse me? There are so many people here I want to speak with."

Zach admits he wasn't at all convinced anything would come out of this second meeting. His wife had the same doubts, asking, "Aren't you worried he might lose that notebook?" He didn't. With Krajina's recommendation, Zach was taken on by the University of British Columbia's Triumf, Canada's National Laboratory for Particle and Nuclear Physics. Eventually he became the facility's head of operations.

Another immigrant with memories of the Krajinas' help from this time is Věra Roller. Because her father had been an official in the Czech National Socialist party (for which he was later imprisoned by the Communists in one of their nefarious concentration camps), the Czechoslovak Association's Vancouver Branch officially sponsored her and her twenty-two-year-old son, Dušan. It proved to be a good choice for the association, with Věra eventually becoming the capable editor of the Czech language newspaper in Toronto, called *Nový Domov* (New Homeland).

The first week in Vancouver Věra and her son Dušan lived with the Krajinas. Marie was a bit shocked by the boy's excessively hirsute appearance, which was de rigueur among recalcitrant Czech youth at the time. True to her ways, Marie gently mentioned (using the endearing diminutive *Dušánek*) that his scraggly beard was no longer in fashion in North America. According to Věra, less than fifteen minutes later *Dušánek* was shaving his beard off. Such was the power not only of Krajina but those nearest to him.

15

Various Battles

ALREADY IN THE SPRING of 1957 Pat Carney reported in the *Vancouver Province* that Krajina had completed a fifteen-month project which established the environmental conditions under which trees grow best in British Columbia. She predicted that this "may very well revolutionize B.C. and Pacific Northwest reforestation methods." To some, this resembled the firing at Fort Sumter — particularly to those who thought that no money should be wasted on reforestation at all.

Much later, in 1970, the year he retired, Krajina told the *Vancouver Province*: "Twenty years ago when I first came to B.C., there were countless trees of 333 feet or so. I myself measured a 270-footer in the Nanaimo area. But they are all gone." He then explained in the newspaper that one of the reasons people of British Columbia had gained so much knowledge about tree growing was that it had virgin forests to study. He pleaded to leave some undisturbed examples for generations to come so that they would be able to study trees in their natural state as well.

Eventually he narrowed his target to forest company management which, according to him, fell short of the management in the neighbouring U.S. In British Columbia it was only 8,000 cubic feet per acre in unmanaged forests, while with proper silviculture the harvest could be 14,000, as in the U.S. "The forest industry talks about proper planting techniques," Krajina concluded, "but those words are something of an empty slogan. Too many companies keep staffs of experts to impress others and do not make proper use of them."

A few days later the chief forester at MacMillan Bloedel waded in with a statement that the MacBlo yield results were good and that comparisons such as Krajina's were meaningless because of the different growing conditions: the U.S. Pacific Northwest had not been glaciated and consequently had an undisturbed, deep rich soil and warmer climate which B.C. lacked.

The *Vancouver Province* did not enter the foray directly, but in the last paragraph of the story noted that Krajina was an internationally recognized authority on silviculture and that he had been recently awarded a citation by the Northwest Scientific Association in recognition of his "outstanding achievements in the field of plant ecology," thereby leaving little doubt whose side of the argument the newspaper favoured.

As a result of his many criticisms of forest practices — the clear-cutting and the slash burning — the companies frequently protested to Krajina's department at the university: first botany, and then later forestry. Some company executives even called for his dismissal. As Krajina was clearly establishing himself as an extremely talented and serious scientist, the forest companies' complaints fell largely on deaf ears. His great supporter was Norman "Larry" MacKenzie. A survivor of the World War I trenches, a graduate of Harvard and Cambridge, he was one of the more illustrious of UBC's presidents, during whose eighteen-year tenure the number of students quadrupled. A member of the Massey Commission, he was also one of the movers behind the establishment of the Canada Council for the Arts.

MacKenzie constituted a power quite equal to the forest company giants of the day, such as MacMillan Bloedel. MacKenzie was also

Krajina's good friend from the United Church. On one occasion when he heard about Krajina's conflict with the forestry companies and the pressure they were applying to the university's Faculty of Forestry, he said to his friend quite plainly: "Don't worry about that Vlady, we'll take care of things for you." And they did. Norman MacKenzie was president until 1962 and by then whatever danger there had been to Krajina of being dismissed had pretty much passed.

✐

In 1966 Krajina assumed his by now familiar verbal battle position during a meeting of the Canadian Plant Society in Vancouver. It came when one of its committees announced that an Ontario forest area near Petawawa was to be its choice of Canada's sylvan study area for the upcoming International Biological Program.

Calling the choice "overwhelmingly illogical" because it would show Canada as a country with poor forest production, Krajina fired his first salvo, saying that unlike Canada, countries such as the U.S. and the Soviet Union would undoubtedly pick their best forest areas for the biological program. The members of the committee defended their choice, claiming that Petawawa was a research forest that already had all the necessary facilities, indicating that, had British Columbia been their choice as Krajina wanted, it would have taken several years to develop them.

Perhaps to placate the angry Krajina, Paul Gorham of the National Research Council, knowing that this was Krajina's specialty, added that the upcoming study would deal not only with productivity but with the complete biological process of the forest environment.

Barely a year later, in September 1967, now well aware of the power of the press in Canada — especially when it came to local affairs — Krajina returned to his favourite subject. Under the headline "Botanist Asks End in Slash Burning," he gave another interview to the *Vancouver Sun*, cunningly choosing a time when much of the province was covered in smoke emanating from its annual September slash burning. Allowing that while all the eye-burning haze was bad enough, he claimed that this was not its worst consequence. Far more important, according to him, was that slash burning destroyed the humus necessary for future growth.

This time his opponent was Victoria's chief forest protection officer, Cy Phillips, who claimed that never had slash burning proven its value more overwhelmingly than in that summer, the summer of 1967, when the fire hazard in the southern part of the province was unusually high. Despite a very dry summer only one major fire had developed. Phillips went on to explain that slash is often the culprit in such fires, acting as kindling and leading to fire among the big trees. He claimed that controlled slash burning prevented that.

To which Krajina replied that he was not against all slash burning, allowing "we have evidence that a limited amount of slash burning is not bad, providing a certain amount of caution is used." But he also rolled out his big guns, suggesting that the law should be changed, forcing the logging companies to pile the slash while cutting down trees. It should then be taken from the dry side of the mountain to the wet side and that burning of it should be delayed until October.

Phillips then brought in the economic argument, which may have been a mistake: "I don't think the industry has the machines or the money to pile up the slash. And if we can't compete in the lumber and pulp markets of the world we might as well as pack up and let it all burn."

It caused Krajina to play his own trump card, a statement which has since become something of the environmentalists' credo. The concern about the future: to Krajina much worse than the haze was the fact that if slash was totally burned off it would probably delay new growth for one hundred years. While today there is no blanket law prohibiting slash burning, there are stringent regulations limiting it, which bring to mind Krajina's words about a "certain amount of caution."

There were also controversies involving specific forest areas, such as the one involving Cathedral Grove on Vancouver Island. The provincial park was established in 1947, three years after lumber magnate H.R. MacMillan donated it to the province — with great fanfare. Nineteen years later Krajina visited the park and came to the conclusion that it really wasn't such a big sacrifice on the part of MacMillan Bloedel.

The giant Douglas fir trees had been scarred by fire already a hundred years ago. As a result they were diseased, which was an open invitation for a fungi invasion and thus they had little or no commercial value. "If a big wind comes along, there'll be nothing left at all," Krajina told the *Vancouver Sun*. The park is also narrow, and thus the large trees along its edges have little protection from high winds.

Perhaps some people thought he was being a bit overly dramatic, but in 2011 the provincial parks website warned to use caution "and stay off the trails on windy days." It also informed the public that the Living Forest Trail is closed because of "significant damage done by a falling tree." Today one can see many trees down as a result of wind storms.

16
Reserves Established

THE YEAR 1970 SAW Vladimir Krajina's official retirement from the University of British Columbia, although in reality he was only being freed from the burden of regular lecturing and from supervising a few graduate students. There were other fairly sizeable fish to fry.

Without Krajina it is highly unlikely there would have been anything resembling the ecological reserves in British Columbia. Certainly not already during the 1970s. Along with his mapping of its biogeoclimatic zones, the ecological reserves of British Columbia were Krajina's enormous contribution to the environment. Among those who have put this province on the map, Krajina ranks right up there with George Vancouver and his exploration of the coastline and Alexander Mackenzie with his crossing of the North American continent.

Granted, Krajina's feat does not at first seem as pioneering as Vancouver's or Mackenzie's. It did not provide an image anywhere nearly as dramatic as the good captain on the deck of his ship with a telescope to his eye, sails fluttering above and canoes full of natives suspiciously watching the scene from a respectful distance. Or that mountain of energy called Mackenzie, making his way through the wilderness until he pushed the last batch of brush aside near Bella Coola. And suddenly there it was — the blue ocean he had been searching for so long — and he could happily paint his "Alex Mackenzie, from Canada, by land, 22nd July 1793" on a nearby rock.

If Krajina had travelled to Clayoquot Sound near Tofino 178 years later, he too could have scribbled his name on a rock there, "Krajina, father of many ecological reserves of which this is the first. It was established due to its great diversity of seabird colonies." Except that by then he was too busy, filling out applications for other reserves, meeting with politicians, bureaucrats, ecologists and journalists — doing anything that would bring the idea of such reserves to the public eye.

Here was not a dramatic sight at all, with Krajina and his students trudging through the rain forest, examining, mapping, evaluating and then, back in his UBC shack, proposing particular reserves to the government of the day.

The idea for the creation of British Columbia's ecological reserves was simple: for scientific studies, tracts of land should be set aside in various locations throughout the province, and these would remain totally undisturbed. But unlike provincial parks, these would not be as readily accessible to the general public, for example, for overnight stays (although fires are not permitted). The official website of B.C. Parks explains the idea's origin as follows: "The Government of British Columbia, encouraged by Krajina . . . and other scientists, agreed in 1968 to form an Ecological Reserve Committee to advise on the selection of potential reserve sites."

Already in the fall of 1969 a Vancouver newspaper reported that a group was laying the "groundwork for undisturbed tracts." It quoted Krajina, "a botanist who is heading a group of scientists interested in the program," as saying that British Columbia leads in Canada and most parts of the world in its establishment of ecological reserves. The article appeared almost two years before the actual passing of the Ecological Reserve Act by the British Columbia Legislature. In it, the highly confident

Krajina at work among his beloved wild flowers while
assessing a potential ecological reserve. (PHOTO: K. KLINKA)

Krajina stated that "European ecologists would be most gratified if they
could recover lands in their virgin state. We fortunately have some parts
of the province where we do not have to spend money to recover the different types of ecosystems."

For a succinct introduction to the intention behind the reserves, one
can do no better than to quote from the 1979 *ForesTalk Resource Magazine*:

One of B.C.'s most spectacular forests, a Sitka spruce stand near Port Chanal in the Queen Charlottes, will never be logged. Nor will man ever interfere with the rare Mara Meadow orchids near Salmon Arm, or the Stone sheep habitat at Gladys Lake on the Spatsizi Plateau. These sites, and 90 others like them, occupy a special position in the province. They have been set aside as ecological reserves. You won't see them advertised anywhere; they aren't marked on any tourist map. However, although a few very fragile reserves are accessible to the public only by special permit, the rest are normally open for such uses as hiking, bird watching and photography, as well as for their prime uses — research and education.

But why go to all the trouble of carefully setting aside these particular parcels of land? Because in each reserve there is something important to preserve. In some cases the special feature is a unique plant, animal or landform; more often it is [an] entire ecosystem typical to a particular region — a complete system of plants, animals and their environment.

Once the ecological reserves began to be established, Krajina sat down at the end of each year to write a report on the work of the Ecological Reserves Committee. He wrote them, but you won't find a word about them in high school history books, which is a pity. In his 1975 progress report on the ecological reserves Krajina mentioned that having been prompted by British Columbia, the provinces of Quebec, Saskatchewan, Manitoba, and New Brunswick have already passed or are about to pass their own ecological reserves acts.

He cast aside his dislike of the Soviets, at least temporarily, in stating that both B.C. and the Soviet Union showed good planning on the ecological reserve front. But then, in typically Krajina-belabored English, he couldn't resist a jab at a power which, for the past eight years, had occupied his native country: "This very high rate in one free society with full political freedoms, where everything develops slowly with participation of all people concerned, and in one country controlled by a dictatorship operating easily with the short-cuts which do not allow any opposing views, are rather a great stimulation for our work in which we cannot become idle or tired or satisfied with any partial success."

Although the provincial legislature passed the Ecological Reserve Act
in 1971, the effective starting point for his ecological reserve campaign
should have really been predated by six years, to November 25, 1965. On
that day in Victoria several academics as well as an official from the Provincial Museum met with Ray Williston, minister of Lands, Forests and
Water Resources.

Williston was informed about the need for the creation of ecological reserves in British Columbia; he was also told that this action was strongly
supported by the International Biological Program in which Canada
was a leading participant. The minister was basically in agreement and
promised to brief other members of the provincial cabinet on the project.
He was handed letters of support from the visiting delegation with reasons given for the need for the creation of the reserves. "Conservation of
all kinds of natural environmental conditions [is] imperative for survival
and maintenance of large heterogeneous natural gene pool of different
organisms," went part of the reasoning. With a hint of editorializing, the
group couldn't resist noting: "This is particularly necessary in a world
whose current tendencies are to simplify, modify, and destroy all that is
not immediately useful to man."

The concluding sentence of that paragraph constituted a bit of a bait
for the Social Credit government of the day, which was usually much
more responsive to proposed economic rather than academic stimuli.
Recognizing that governments were never averse to the idea of leaving
a larger imprint on provincial history, the group added: "The diversity
of life in the natural biogeocoenoses and their biogeoclimatic zones is a
national and international treasure which should remain available forever."

Exactly a year later, an organization with a mouthful of a name —
Terrestrial Communities Subcommittee of the Canadian Committee of
the International Biological Program — met in Victoria. Consisting of
elected government officials and representatives of provincial government departments plus various academics, the committee laid important
groundwork for the idea of ecological reserves.

Early the following year Krajina chaired a Vancouver meeting of
twenty-nine prominent scientists who were informed of the survey work

about to be undertaken, with an eye to the establishment of the reserves. The work was completed a year later, when Williston and W.K. Kiernan, minister of Recreation and Conservation, agreed to "the formation of the British Columbia Government Ecological Reserves Committee."

Krajina was named one of the co-chairmen of the committee with the right to co-opt other scientists "who would actively participate in the work of ecological reserves." In his report on subsequent meetings he stated that twenty to fifty people were now usually present at the meetings as interest in the reserves grew.

Krajina taking photos,
the Nass River, 1972.
(PHOTO: K. KLINKA)

Early in 1971, during the throne debate at the Victoria legislature, Williston presented the results of several years of study and announced that an Ecological Reserves Bill would be presented during the upcoming session of the legislature. It was duly passed in April.

Not everyone in private industry or government circles fully understood the function of the proposed reserves. Alistair Crerar, director of the Government Land Use Committee Secretariat, suggested including former garbage dump sites among the proposed ecological reserves, to which Krajina patiently explained that of primary interest to those proposing the reserves was "to find out how nature operated normally without human beings."

In the end, Krajina was elated with the passage of the bill, although there must have been some who were not. Section 5 of the bill stated that any area designated as an ecological reserve would automatically be removed from disposition as granted under other legislation such as the Land Act, Grazing Act, Water Act, Mineral Act, Placer-Mines Act, Coal Act, Petroleum and Natural Gas Act, Water Resources Act, or Mines Rights-of-way Act.

From that wording, one would assume that the needs of the Ecological Reserves Act would automatically push aside any other proposed use of selected land. Such was far from the case. Before the year 1972 was over, Krajina had a thick folder of correspondence from D. Bothwick, deputy minister of the provincial Ministry of Lands, Forests and Water Resources. In essence, these were rejection slips, with which all authors are thoroughly familiar. But while the literary kind often proffer the mysterious claim that the sent manuscript does not fit into the publisher's program, Krajina's ecological rejection slips were never that vague. For example, his proposal for Ecological Reserve No. 93, at Chewhat Lake and Climax Forest, was rejected, not only because it encompassed several mineral claims but because it also lay within an area to be included in the proposed Pacific Rim National Park.

And up north, proposal number 82 at Murray Range near Pine Pass was in conflict with Amoco Canada's natural gas permit. The wording of the rejection of Krajina's proposal number 76 at Morfee Lake within the Municipality of MacKenzie was even more blunt, stating that "the acreage requested was far too ambitious. Moreover, the land requested was required by the local community for recreation." As an added reason for the rejection slip, Bothwick noted that "the proposal was strongly objected to by Takla Forest Products Ltd, Peace Salvage Association and The District of Mackenzie . . . ," among others.

Proposal number 74 at Becker's Prairie was turned down because: (1) a major part of it was within the boundaries of government of Canada's terrain used for military purposes; (2) it was used for grazing of 2,700 head of cattle from four local ranches, and (3) it was heavily used by waterfowl hunters in the fall.

Proposal number 31 for the Kerouard Islands, part of the Haida Gwaii archipelago, was rejected because, since 1916, the islands had been reserved by the Federal Department of Transport.

Some proposals had been turned down simply because they had "natural gas potential." Others were rejected because it was questioned whether they really had the potential for hydrological studies, as Krajina claimed. And proposal number 70 for Horsey Creek in the McBride Area reserve was rejected "because no outstanding dense stand of Western Red

Cedar was detected in the area as claimed by the examining surveyor."

Nevertheless, in 1972 Krajina proudly reported that he had spoken about "this excellent environmental development" at scientific meetings in Greece, India, Indonesia, Jamaica, and Australia. "Everywhere the message was greatly applauded because of the great foresight by the British Columbia provincial government."

Such was the good news. But there was also the other kind. Krajina recognized that "certain very important ecosystems . . . could not be covered by the new Ecological Reserve Act because they are no longer in Crown lands." He knew that it was "necessary to preserve them as soon as possible, if we wish to prevent their possible total destruction." Clearly it wasn't always possible.

Nevertheless, by 1972 there were forty-three ecological reserves in existence, ranging in size from 0.6 hectares to 6,212 hectares. The previous year Krajina had presented his progress report at what to this day counts as the grandest provincial gathering of notables concerning the reserves. Arranged by Leon Koerner, it was attended by the chancellors of Simon Fraser and UBC, the president of UBC and a representative of the University of Victoria. While those guests were expected to attend, somewhat surprising was the presence of a representative from the Council of Forest Industries of B.C. as well as that of British Columbia Forest Products. What's more, a year later Krajina was made fellow of the Institute of Forestry of Canada, a sure sign that the forestry giants had finally recognized the importance of his work.

In 1975 he told a botany seminar at UBC that there were now fifty-nine reserves covering 104,073 acres, while 235 proposals have been presented to the government so far, "although we don't expect that out of every proposal we'll get a reserve." He also criticized the Fish and Wildlife Branch of the provincial government for opposing a proposal for the Toad Hotsprings reserve, site of a natural saltlick which attracted large numbers of animals. "It's very disappointing," he said. "These are the people who should be proposing the area [for a reserve] on their own." And why? Krajina explained that animals approaching salt licks are docile and easily stalked. Hunting near them should not be allowed as it would be entirely unsporting.

When the *Vancouver Sun* reported on the seminar, Krajina responded with a letter, saying it should be stressed that the proposed reserves include not only lands with rich and fertile soils but also those with low or even negligible productivity because they too needed to be preserved.

In the same letter he corrected the newspaper's statement that access to the reserves would be limited to authorized persons, saying that there is no intention to do so. However, there needed to be strict observance of the necessary regulations. These should include no camping (except perhaps with special permission), no fires, and no destruction of natural phenomena. The general tone of the letter showed that by that time Krajina was well aware that the press was generally on his side, and he praised the newspaper for informing the public about efforts to preserve parts of the province in its natural state.

At present the number of ecological reserves in this province continues to grow, albeit much more slowly than in Krajina's time. In 2011 there were 148 of them. None approved during the last twelve years is anywhere near in size to Gladys Lake Reserve, created in 1975 on the Spatsizi Plateau with its 40,541 hectares. Or the Checleset Bay Reserve on Northern Vancouver Island, created in 1981, measuring 35,592 hectares.

Nowadays the Ministry of Environment spokesman reports that at present the average size of a reserve is 1,084 hectares and that, unlike at the outset, there is no person specifically in charge of the reserve program. As to why the growth of the system has lately achieved a snail's pace, the government's answer is an ambiguous statement that "the land use planning process is nearly done."

A somewhat clearer statement comes from one of Krajina's students, who later became a member of the Ecological Reserves Board, Dr. Bruce Fraser. Here is his assessment of the reserves' history:

> In the early years, his [Krajina's] lobbying of government was extensive and insistent. Government barely understood the scientific rationale for large reserves but his persuasiveness prevailed. Later, the bureaucracy, heeding economic signals from senior government derived from successful lobbying by industry, progressively minimized the size of reserves. They tended to become postage stamps of rare

species and plant associations rather than the significant scientific benchmarks that Vladimir believed were necessary for the long term understanding of the productive forest on which a healthy industry was based. The contest was always about losing immediate logging opportunity vs science for the long term. One of his most famous cautionary public lectures began with "I see Vancouver a ghost town". . . as he went on to explain how much of the city depended on the health and productivity of the forest and its industries and the ultimate dangers of failure to learn and conserve.

Krajina on a field trip around Prince George examining
a biological specimen, c. 1978. (PHOTO: O. SLAVIK)

Krajina gesturing to a colleague while laying out a potential
ecological reserve in central B.C., c. 1975. (PHOTO: O. SLAVIK)

There were various specific reasons for setting up reserves. Among
the most bizarre is the relationship between the ponderosa pine and rattle snake dens which can be found at the Kalamalka Lake Reserve near
Vernon. Needless to say, access here is limited by nature itself.

A more romantic raison d'être is offered by the San Juan Ridge Ecological Reserve east of Port Renfrew on Vancouver Island, which boasts
a profusion of the rare white avalanche lily, or, as Vladimir Krajina
would say, *Erythronium montanum*. There is also the Skagit River

Reserve with its stand of Pacific rhododendron. Or, still speaking of romance, there is the seabird and marine mammal breeding area at Byers/Conroy/Harvey/Sinnet Islands at Hecate Strait.

On the largest reserve, Gladys Lake Ecological Reserve on the Spatsizi Plateau, there are stone sheep, mountain goats and caribou. And while the Chasm Reserve near Clinton features ponderosa pine at its northern limit, the Checleset Bay Ecological Reserve provides habitat for the province's prime sea otter population.

Other reserves preserve breeding colonies of herring and ring-billed gulls, native oysters, endangered Vancouver Island marmots, northern adder's-tongue fern, well-developed lichen communities, a stand of Garry oaks or the most arid ecosystem in Canada. In the Kootenays there is the fairly large Lew Creek Ecological Reserve, which is unique in that it preserves three biogeoclimatic zones in the same drainage basin.

There may also be some reserves whose reasons for existence are less clear. When Krajina arrived on an island off Horseshoe Bay during the early seventies to examine a proposed reserve, the student with him was somewhat wary of the proposal. The idea of creating a reserve of fairly common Douglas fir in the dry subzone of western hemlock was unusual and could have been a scheme of some well-to-do local residents to create a buffer zone between their properties and the rest of the island. Since there was no suggestion that a bribe was involved, Krajina was not about to look a gift horse in the mouth. Any proposal for a new reserve was welcome, especially this one, so close to a major metropolitan area. Despite the suspected bad omen of Krajina dislocating his ankle while examining the landscape, the result was reserve number 48, on Bowen Island.

In 1973 came the establishment of the Vladimir J. Krajina (Port Chanal) Ecological Reserve on Haida Gwaii, which at the time was still called the Queen Charlotte Islands. A windy, storm-prone place on the western side of Graham Island, it extends from the coast to the majestic ridges. At one point the terrain rises to 825 metres, with steep slopes facing the inlet while moderate to flat terrain exists elsewhere.

It is a classic ecological reserve location, with a genetic bank of rare as well as common species. Calling it "a benchmark ecosystem," the

Friends of Ecological Reserves literature goes on to say: "Here is an outdoor museum and laboratory available for botanical, wildlife, and geographical fishery." As memorials go, this reserve on Haida Gwaii is an excellent one. Accessible only by boat or float plane, the reserve consists of 9,734 hectares with abundant fauna and flora. In other words, it is one of the larger and more varied ones within the system, including sixty kilometres of marine shoreline with large islands and a fjord at Port Chanal. There is one relatively large body of fresh water, Mercer Lake, and several smaller lakes on Hippa Island. The entire watershed of Mace Creek as well as several minor creeks are also part of the reserve.

Krajina must have loved the reserve's mossy underlay with luxuriant, almost pure stands of Sitka spruce. But there are also barren headlands, meadows, bogs and alpine habitats which extend to unusually low elevations. The reserve has an abundance of liverworts and mosses, which Krajina, being an avid bryologist, must have appreciated as well. In fact some 130 species of plants exist on the reserve, many of them endemic to the islands or provincially rare.

Among the bird population, significant colonies of ancient murrelets, Cassin's auklets and both Leach and fork-tailed storm petrels inhabit the reserve. Also present are bald eagles and peregrine falcons. The Queen Charlotte subspecies of northern saw-whet owl, Steller's jay and hairy woodpecker make their home within the reserve and about three hundred Steller's sea lions use Hippa Island as a winter haulout. The Mercer Lake system is crucial to eight thousand sockeye salmon with coho, pink and chum salmon also present.

Nevertheless, all is not well within the remote Vladimir J. Krajina Reserve, with climate change being considered the greatest threat to its abundant nature. Habitat loss due to a raised sea level and increased storm activity along the already stormy shoreline poses a threat to the shorebirds' nesting habits. The expected warming of the sea and, with it, changed patterns of runoff from the island pose another threat along with possible drought conditions.

Other threats include commercial fishing, poaching and logging activity in the neighborhood of the reserve, which endangers the sockeye salmon. Also preying raccoons and even flight traffic disrupt the

Krajina with his ice-axe, c. 1978.

seabird's nesting habits. At present these are merely threats, many of which are faced elsewhere in the province and throughout the world. All in all, Vladimir Krajina would have been happy with the pristine reserve that bears his name.

∽

Even with all his research and lobbying on behalf of the reserves, Krajina still found time to actively oppose the scheduled visit to Vancouver of the Soviet premier, Alexei Kosygin, who had earlier been assaulted in Eastern Canada by a Hungarian exile. The day before his visit in 1971 some two thousand demonstrators marched through Vancouver with placards. Krajina was in the forefront. The *Vancouver Province* had published a letter, in which Krajina in his inimitable style advises the Soviet premier what to do: "He should introduce in Soviet Russia and countries under Soviet control the only democratic way for self-determination, i.e. by free voting to decide where and under what political regime they wish to live. Such free voting should be under the supervision of the United Nations." The letter was signed by him as president of the Vancouver Chapter of the Czechoslovak National Association.

Alas, there was no reaction. Despite his advice, the Soviet Union did not manage to dissolve itself until twenty years later. Yet there was at least one tangible result to the visit and the protest. The film *Russian Roulette* was based on the novel *Kosygin Is Coming* by the Canadian author Tom Ardies. It was released in 1975, and had the distinction of having in it Louise Fletcher, who won an Oscar that year. Unfortunately, not for *Russian Roulette*, which was called "a violent, unsatisfying thriller," but for a much better film, *One Flew over the Cuckoo's Nest*. Its director, the Czech-born Miloš Forman, received one too.

A year later Krajina's foray into politicized economics in the *Vancouver Province* was equally unsuccessful. Here Krajina tore into labour unions under the title "How Can We Tolerate This Strike Extortion?" In it, he argued that we were living in a "hyperdemocratic state, which dangerously approaches anarchy," and then went on to establish the principle that while almost everybody wanted higher wages or salaries, which would supposedly mean a better standard of living, almost nobody cared what the result would be. That result, according to him, would be "constant inflation."

He concluded: "Governmental control of income and prices can be done justly for all concerned. . . . Such governments will be solidly backed by all good common sense people who will unite when requested to do so." It was an unusual thought from a man who had suffered government control in the hands of two extremely powerful totalitarian regimes, although he did mention that his solution applied only to those governments which were democratically elected.

The *Vancouver Province* article may not have been particularly well constructed, but it did once more indicate Krajina's undying faith in innate human goodness. Despite his own personal experiences, Krajina seemed to believe the individual would do the right thing, if only given a chance.

Elsewhere in his writings Krajina defended the idea of private enterprise in forestry, hinting that competition guaranteed no company would become excessively powerful. But obviously, according to him, this principle should not be applied indiscriminately. It should also be remembered that he had been the general secretary of the Czech National *Socialist* Party.

The decade was also the time for many accolades and honours to be lavished on Krajina. In 1970 came the Northwest Scientific Association's citation for "outstanding work in northwest ecology" and in 1972 the Lawson Medal for a Lifetime Contribution to Botany in Canada from the Canadian Botanical Association. A year later he received his first honorary degree. Inscribed in Krajina's beloved Latin, it came from the now defunct Notre Dame University in Nelson, B.C. In 1979 the National Film Board made a movie about him entitled *The Forests and Vladimir Krajina*.

17

Student Relations

ALREADY IN PRE-WAR times his friends were impressed by Vladimir Krajina's warm interaction with his students, starting with those who worked with him in the High Tatras, classifying the local flora. While out on these field trips, especially to the Votruba Hut, which has already been mentioned, the students were frequently called upon to follow Krajina in unusual duties. When, as it frequently happened, inclement weather brought in unexpected visitors, these had to be fed by Krajina's older sister who was in charge of the kitchen. Sometimes the number of boarders reached as high as twenty. It was at such times that the agile Krajina and his students, equipped with enormous rucksacks, would descend into the valley to buy supplies, then make their way back to the hut like chamois sheep — inclement weather or not. This required considerable effort, but people who were there witnessed a student devotion to their professor which was second to none.

Later in German-occupied Czechoslovakia, Krajina bravely led his students in public demonstrations. And when the Nazis closed the universities, many enthusiastically repaid him by performing courier and other duties for the nascent Resistance movement.

Loyalty to a professor is not that rare in Canada either, although it's more frequent in the natural sciences such as geology and botany. Such studies require frequent field trips, often lasting for several days if not weeks. A former head of UBC's research forest, Jack Walters, who had earlier been a Krajina student, claims that "Krajina was the essence of what a university teacher should be. He always talked directly to the student."

At times his message could be potentially dangerous, as recounted in the 1978 National Film Board movie *The Forests and Vladimir Krajina*. One of Krajina's students explained: "I camped with Vladimir and a group of his students one summer about twenty-six years ago. . . . Vladimir would return triumphantly, I am afraid, with a satchel of edible mushrooms — he said. He made mushroom soup for us. It was kind of him, I suppose. He said the scientific name for the mushrooms was bolitis sock-it-to-us. Four pounds of bolitis sock-it-to-us, two quarts of water and a pinch of salt. After we'd had a few sips Vladimir would say — in his flawless English: 'Dze gut dzing about bolitis sock-it-to-us vaz dzat from two to tree daiz dze effect duz not take of dze poison.'"

Another veteran of those trips remembers that Krajina would often say, "The best place to learn about ecology was not in class but in the forest. The forest," he would add, "is a textbook." He recalls that Krajina "loved to take the students out into the forest textbook. He expected that we would know the names of all plants we saw. One time we tried to catch him out: we started climbing up a mountain and while still barely above sea level we collected a few samples of mosses. And when we got much higher we asked him: 'Look at this moss, Professor Krajina. Can you tell what it is?'"

"Sure I can," he answered without batting an eye. "That's the stuff you collected down there at the parking lot."

In a Czech documentary film about Krajina, another of his students, Hamish Kimmins, who later became a noted British Columbia forest ecologist himself, eloquently told how Krajina taught him to view nature as an "ecological theatre." In a theatre there is a stage, the play and also the actors. The scenery on such an ecological stage consists of the soil, climate, topography and things like a forest fire.

According to Kimmins, Krajina drew an extremely valuable map of the ecological stages of British Columbia, in which each stage designates the type of drama that will be produced on it. These dramatic moments consist of sudden natural events such as high winds or forest fires. Those of us who are in the audience, he explained, can follow their effects. We can do this, of course, only until the next storm or blaze comes. These phases are akin to the acts in a theatrical drama. The plants and animals that are involved constitute the actors — members of a theatre company who in time are replaced by new generations. In other words, Krajina "created a map of various theatre stages with whose help we are now able to describe the ecological dramas and that constitute the basic framework of work leading to maintaining biodiversity." Elsewhere, Kimmins concluded that Krajina was "a prophet, but few listened. . . . I have fantastic admiration for him. . . . He was the Churchill of the forest ecology world. He had vision, energy surpassing anyone else, commitment and a sense of social responsibility."

Krajina understood that forests composed of old growth create many valuable environments for animals: for the bears for example, or for the fish that swim in streams to and from the ocean. They all make use of the big trees, even those that die and fall onto the forest floor or into the rivers where they produce the right conditions for biodiversity — all part of the drama.

Another enthusiastic former student is Patrick Moore, something of a revisionist environmentalist, who suggests he could be called a Greenpeace dropout. In his book *Trees Are the Answer*, Moore recalls his moment of enlightenment: "It was not until one day in my second year of university (in the Faculty of Forestry, naturally), that I began to gain an intellectual understanding of the great web of life that I had been immersed in all my childhood. The occasion was a noon-hour lecture by Dr. Vladimir Krajina, the founder of the British Columbia Ecological Reserves and the author of the classification system for all British Columbia ecosystems. It was a lecture that changed my life."

Moore goes on to explain that Krajina "shocked him into attention" by making him realize the circumstances of his own existence and intuitive knowledge that ecology was not merely the study of food chains and nutrient cycles, but an innovative way to look at our surroundings and the miracle of creation. At that moment he realized it was possible to link rational thought with spiritual wonder, also that through seeing nature as a whole, one could understand many things about the mystery of life.

Moore credits Krajina with enlarging his awareness so that he was no longer an agnostic who saw science as merely a technical subject. It was here that his transformation from a mere forestry student into a prominent ecologist really began.

Dr. Karel Klinka, Krajina's last graduate
student, inspecting a plant.

Of all Krajina's students, the closest to him probably was Karel Klinka, a Czech who came to Canada in 1969 with the wave of post-invasion refugees. Although a forester by training, he spent the first two years in Terrace, B.C., as a manual labourer. There he kept hearing about a man named Krajina at UBC and eventually went to Vancouver to talk to the venerable professor. Despite Krajina's official retirement, Klinka was taken on as one of Krajina's last graduate students, earning his master's degree a year later, eventually continuing on to a PhD. Klinka surmises that perhaps Krajina took him on, even after his official retirement, because "he wanted to have someone to follow in his footsteps." He explains how Krajina "cleared a table for me in his army hut. I shared a room with his Hawaiian plant collection, and he was constantly worried about the plants. You see, at the time I was a heavy smoker and he was afraid that one day his entire collection would go up in smoke." Also in the hut was Krajina's secretary of many years, Mrs. Svoboda, and his two remaining graduate students — one was from Calgary, the other from Japan.

Klinka quickly recognized some of the professorial traits he had previously seen in other European pedagogues: "He always behaved like a professor. He was reserved. Only towards the end of our relationship did he finally say that I could call him Vladimir. Before that it was always Doctor or Professor Krajina."

According to Klinka, Krajina had a strong conviction that the results of his research were always final. For example, it came to him as something of a shock that on occasion the boundaries of the biogeoclimatic zones he had set during the early 1970s were being questioned, and he became quite angry about it. But Klinka says that towards him Krajina never showed anything but patience, occasionally providing him with valuable advice and even exclusive botany lectures. He was generous with his time. Klinka often had trouble identifying pieces of moss, an area of botany in which Krajina was an expert. Klinka collected them in envelopes, which he stored inside some fifty shoeboxes, and Krajina spent about a month correctly identifying each one for him.

Sometimes Krajina would take him on special one-on-one field trips. "I would walk behind him, he would pick up a plant, ask me what its name was. Usually I said I didn't know. He would tell me and then he would hand it to me and I would put it in my bag. That's why I didn't take many pictures during those excursions. I was too busy."

Klinka saw the B.C. forests, which form 90 percent of the area of B.C., as an ideal environment for Krajina. "Every bit of Central European forests had been analyzed. Here it was exactly the opposite. It was something of a *terra incognita*."

⁓

By the 1980s Krajina was no longer involved with purely scientific research. His priority was the ecological reserves. For every new proposal for the creation of a reserve, there had to be a file of about fifty pages with the description of its vegetation, for which Krajina used primarily Latin names. When asked for its common name he would often readily produce it, but sometimes he couldn't. Many mosses and lichens don't even have such names.

According to Klinka, Latin simply didn't work here in Canada: "Czech names are nice . . . charming. English names are not so nice, but they are often used, though they tend to sound somewhat awkward. But Latin was his forte. You should see the names Krajina gave to plant communities! Sometimes they ran for three or four lines. No one could spell them, let along pronounce them. . . . And on top of every other inconvenience, the Americans have a certain aversion towards Latin."

Guides to the various plants were eventually produced by the Forestry Ministry where Klinka later found employment. They were written in simple English with graphs showing rates of growth and other factors which could be understood by people who made decisions in the field. They were then copied and reproduced by other Canadian provinces and American states.

At least indirectly, another Krajina legacy was in the establishment of the principle that each forester entrusted with making decisions in the field had to be able to identify about one hundred plants, because these are the primary indicators of soil conditions.

Several times Krajina proudly mentioned to Klinka that he was one of the first botanists who insisted on studying plants together with soil and climate. As has been seen, this made him one of the early ecologists in Europe. Even his PhD dissertation has several parts, of which the first deals with plants, the second with soil and climate.

Klinka recalls that Krajina was a tireless worker, and how "even after he retired he couldn't stay home. He always drove his car to the hut where he had his office, and his wife would have to make at least three phone calls to get him to come for lunch." Still, Klinka could see that Krajina was slowing down. Although he was exceptionally agile, even later in life when he became somewhat stocky, there had been a couple of accidents as he ran about the countryside. During a trip to Bowen Island he had badly sprained his leg. A potentially serious accident occurred on Lake Cowichan. Stepping out of a seaplane, Krajina slipped, fell into the water and immediately went under. Fortunately Klinka and others quickly pulled him out, but the incident could have had serious consequences — Krajina was a non-swimmer. He had also broken his leg earlier while bicycling, and when a celebration of the passing of the Ecological Reserves Act was being held in the Faculty Club of the University of British Columbia, he tripped over a rug while rushing to meet some prominent guests. He fell and re-broke it. But no one noticed. Still the legendary hero, he welcomed his guests, then quietly stole away to hail a taxi to take him to the hospital.

This time, however, the leg took longer to heal, and Krajina, without his trips through the forests, was becoming depressed. His ever-resourceful family then planned a trip across Europe and North Africa to distract him. It did the trick: perhaps he didn't emerge from the experience as good as new, but well enough to continue with his field work.

18

Becoming Known

THROUGHOUT HIS CAREER, Krajina's work was widely written about in scientific journals, but the general public was left mostly in the dark about the wealth of his achievements — both in the forest and in the Czech Resistance. Except, of course, for an occasional short newspaper article.

This was especially true until the 1980s, partially because the Czechoslovak Communist regime remained silent about both. Also because his dramatic case, once discussed so eloquently in the British House of Lords, had now receded into history. Churchill was long dead, the exceedingly hot world war had been replaced by a long-lasting and generally undramatic cold one. And botany had never been exactly in the forefront of journalistic interest.

That is why a 1982 article in the *Vancouver Sun* by Agnes Thom constituted something of a revolutionary endeavour. Entitled "Vladimir Krajina: The Spy Who Saved Our Forests," it featured a large portrait of the man with trees or stumps all around it. In places these were inexplicably replaced by chess figures, a fleeing skier and for some strange reason even an inverted Czechoslovak flag. The piece ran in two installments on successive weekends.

Thom recounted Krajina's European adventures, stating that "when they make the big movie of his life — as someone undoubtedly will — they will have enough war, suspense, tragedy and intrigue to satisfy the most sensation-hungry tastes." Then she told about the previous year's Banff conference, attended by forest ministers or their deputies from nine provinces as well as the top officials of major forest companies. She quoted one report that called it a major turnaround in forest management in Canada. Much of the article discussed Krajina's teaching over the previous thirty-two years.

Thom claimed that shortly after Krajina arrived in the province and began spreading his then radical views about existing forest practices, many professors, foresters and industry managers secretly agreed with him. One of them even confessed this to Krajina himself, but then he quickly added: "If you quote me, I'll deny I ever said it!" Obviously what was sorely needed in the equation was Krajina's fearlessness.

Dr. Karel Klinka, Krajina's former student, was asked by Thom to explain the significance of Krajina's classification system for the layman. Klinka obliged: "If something happens to your car and you tell your mechanic it's yellow, a compact, and a two-door, you give him useless information. But if you say it's a 1971 Ford Maverick, the mechanic knows immediately which manual and tools to use to fix it. If you tell me about an area fifty miles east of Hope in a beautiful valley, I don't know too much, but if you talk in terms of its classification, I know exactly what you're talking about and we can make management decisions about that area."

Towards the end of her piece, Thom managed to connect Krajina's two homelands when she talked about slash burning, which Krajina considered a serious problem in British Columbia. The practice, according to him, had been against the law for one hundred and fifty years in Czechoslovakia and he was shocked to find so much of it when he arrived here.

Jan Drabek, the author, interviewing Krajina for a
Czech exile magazine in 1982.

She concluded by saying: "Krajina still begins every talk, every speech
with words which acknowledge his love of freedom and democracy, his
appreciation for being in Canada. He will say, "We are fortunate to be
in a country where we can say what we think."

A year earlier in the magazine *ForesTalk* Krajina explained that when
he came to Canada he was a much younger man with a young man's
ideas. And while he was not necessarily rebellious, he was not happy
with certain forestry practices like slash burning: "Everyone knows you
need humus in your garden. I was even told by Mr. Clyne, one of the
tycoons of MacMillan Bloedel, 'I can't understand the foresters who
burn humus, while I have to apply it in my own garden.'" His great admirer, Hamish Kimmins, claimed that Krajina had a message for chief
foresters: he said that if they were doing in Europe what they practised
in this province they would be thrown in jail.

By the 1980s Krajina had enough stature to be no longer easily assail-
able. Earlier in the year that the Thom story appeared in the *Vancouver
Sun*, Krajina was admitted to the Order of Canada. While he was naturally proud to be so honoured by his adopted country, he was privately

puzzled by the fact he received merely the lowest level of the order.

This was not necessarily vanity. While it is usually noted that he played a giant part in understanding and preserving the ecology of British Columbia, in fact many other Canadian provinces had followed B.C.'s example. Obviously in Ottawa they weren't listening very intently. For the federal government not to have considered his wartime achievements wasn't quite fair either. His help was for the Allies, a victorious club of which both Canada and Czechoslovakia were prominent members.

That same year, the Czech community in this country was treated to an interview with Krajina in which he explained that in 1948 the Canadian recruiters were the first to look him up while he was still in Great Britain. They offered him a teaching position, possibly in British Columbia, which he already knew quite a bit about. He said he was well aware of the tremendous natural wealth available here, and as a botanist he was sure this would have some great advantages. When the Americans came with an offer some time later he told them he had already decided to go to Canada. He never regretted it, concluding the interview by saying: "In reality everything I had set out to do, especially scientifically speaking, I have been able to achieve here."

Here was obviously a man now much more at ease with himself. His example was used by the Czech-Canadian writer Josef Škvorecký at a Toronto conference called The Writer and Human Rights, among whose participants were Nadine Gordimer, Margaret Atwood and Susan Sontag. Škvorecký put it as follows:

> Since individualistic Anglo-Saxons usually demand concrete, individual examples, let me offer you a few. In Canada there lives an old professor by the name of Vladimir Krajina. He teaches at the University of British Columbia in Vancouver and is an eminent botanist who has received high honours from the Canadian government for his work in the preservation of Canadian flora. But in World War II, he was also a most courageous anti-Nazi fighter. . . . Immediately after the Communist coup in 1948, Professor Krajina had to go into hiding again, and he eventually fled the country. Why? Because the Communists had never forgotten that he had warned the Czech underground against cooperating with the Communists. And he was

right: he was not the only one to flee. Hundreds of other anti-Nazi fighters were forced to leave the country, and those who would not or could not ended up on the gallows, in concentration camps, or, if they were lucky, in menial jobs. Among them were many Czech RAF pilots who had distinguished themselves in the Battle of Britain and then had returned to the republic for whose democracy they had risked their lives. All this is a story since repeated in other Central and East European states. It is still being repeated in Cuba, in Vietnam, in Angola, and most recently in Nicaragua.

Škvorecký disagrees somewhat with Černý on the subject of Krajina's willingness to work with the Communists for a common cause (see p. 82). Here one tends to favour Černý's version. After all, he was directly involved with Krajina during the war.

ℐ&

With today's profusion of ecologists of all denominations who warn us about the need for sustainability, we sometimes forget that not too long ago it was generally believed that the world's resources were infinite.

Krajina and his wife Marie with Chancellor J.V. Cline in 1982 after receiving an honorary degree from UBC.

That, especially in a place like British Columbia, no amount of clear-cutting and slash burning could change the fact there would always be more new growth — or "fibre" as they were wont to call trees.

Krajina should be credited with not only challenging this way of thinking but meticulously showing an alternative. In his 1972 MacMillan Lecture in Forestry, he used the opportunity to stress the all-important role of a system in which well-managed forest companies compete with each other "inspired by the best future forest programmes" since, according to Krajina, such a system constitutes the basis of a democratic life. He claimed that having only one privately owned company was no better than a state-owned system,

At the same time in the lecture, however, he argued for a greatly enhanced role of the forester who should be allowed by his company to speak out whenever he senses danger to the environment. In this connection, Krajina quoted from a recent speech by Ray Williston, provincial minister of Lands, Forests and Water Resources. "From the practical point of view the forester is going to have to use his training to manage forests as he has never managed them before. . . . And he is going to have to recognize the fact that he no longer can be exclusively concerned with the volume. . . . He is going to have to concern himself with a type of forest management for industrial use that is concurrent with public use of the same land in terms of recreation, ecological reserves and wilderness areas. Every aspect of his professional training must be brought to the fore, and the faculties of forestry in our universities must accept their share of the responsibility in gaining an understanding of this need." In concluding his speech, Krajina suggested that foresters should be made to take a new oath which would show this new philosophy, and this would elevate them to one of the most respected professions in this country

By the 1980s the Krajina name was becoming readily recognized. The time was fast approaching when even people in his native land would discuss the accomplishments of this hero of two continents. It had been kept from them for over four decades.

19

Happy Returns

IN THE MIDDLE OF November 1989, the Prague anti-government demonstrations began to grow in size and the dissident groups coalesced into the Citizens' Forum. By the end of the month half a million people had braved the bitter cold at Letná Hill to signal the regime that its days were numbered. Finally a new government was named, and the one-time prominent dissident who had become the new minister of Foreign Affairs, met with his Austrian counterpart to symbolically cut the barbed wire at the border.

Late in December, Václav Havel, the largely unknown dissident recently out of prison, was elected president of the Czechoslovak Republic. The Velvet Revolution was complete. Vladimir Krajina's last foe — the Communist Party — had been defeated.

Far away on the northwest shores of the Pacific, the Czechoslovak community had been growing increasingly excited. The entire Krajina household watched somewhat incredulously as the events unfolded on television. Krajina's Czech National Socialists were being reborn with a special congress scheduled for March 1990. It would include the reunion of the exiled branch of the party with the home one. In order to provide a semblance of democracy, the section in Prague had been allowed to lead a miserable existence in the shadow and under total control of the Communist Party.

Despite the fact that Krajina had become somewhat frail with age (he now walked with a cane and needed help with washing and shaving), and despite Marie's bad heart, enthusiastic plans were being made for a triumphant return to the country whose rulers had for forty-one years dragged the Krajina name through the mud. The whole family would return: Krajina and Marie as well as daughter Milena and Vladimir junior, who was now a forty-two-year-old medical doctor, specializing in emergency procedures at the Burnaby General Hospital. He had never been back to his native country since he left it when six months old.

The night before their departure Marie called her son and asked him to come over. When he did, he found his mother in sad shape. He quickly diagnosed her as having atrial fibrillation. "I feel like I am going to die," she confided in him simply. Although he knew that patients who uttered such words were frequently the most competent people to assess the situation, he decided to wait until next morning. The condition could have been brought on by the excitement and might convert to normal on its own just as quickly. Still, he went back home worried, telling her to call him the minute she woke up.

But all was well the next day. Better anyway. On the way to the airport Marie was munching on a banana. As they waited to board the plane she commented that she was already looking forward to coming home. Somewhat surprised, everyone realized she meant returning to Vancouver, not arriving in Prague.

In 1990 the difference between Marxist and Western Europe was sadly noticeable at first glance. Throughout the Federal Republic of Germany the four- or six-lane freeways criss-crossed each other, periodically interrupted by an island with a clean, modern cafeteria-style restaurant. The big change came at the Czech border town of

The Krajina family at the Vancouver Airport en route
to Prague, March 1990.

Rozvadov, where a sprawling complex dominated the crossing. From
there the road to Prague was an old-fashioned two-lane highway. The
one real freeway in the country led eastward from Prague, certainly not
to the border with West Germany. It had been built not to accommo-
date the motoring public but the Russian tanks and truck transports
which would have to be rushed to the border to confront the supposedly
aggressive forces of NATO. The defensive line of the Warsaw Pact was
just to the west of Prague.

Milena remembers that already upon landing in Frankfurt, Krajina
noticed that he had forgotten his hearing aid at home. The family
picked up their rental car and headed east towards the Czechoslovak
border, which is about four hours away — particularly if you stop in
Bavaria for coffee and *kuchen* with whipped cream. As the Krajinas
neared the border, the scene inside the car became more and more emotional. After all, it had been forty-two years! The Czech guards were
pleasant, although their Soviet-style uniforms reminded everyone that
freedom was still young and perhaps even a fragile child.

Silently the older Krajinas watched as the road shrank into a narrow two-lane highway ruled by the decidedly unruly East European drivers. Alongside the highway, the neglected buildings and ugly clusters of panel-housing dominated the scene. The elder Krajinas remembered it from pre-war times as a countryside full of picturesque farm houses and charming villages. Although in 1945 these had in places shown the ravages of war, they were quickly repaired. But six years of a world war couldn't match the devastation of four decades of Communist rule. Abolish private ownership and you've abolished the maintenance which accompanies it.

They stopped for lunch in the town of Plzeň (Pilsen), famous for its beer. Marie, still not 100 percent, surprised the restaurant staff by addressing them in English.

Krajina's mind was mostly on the speech he would be making at the party congress, but these thoughts receded once they entered Prague. It too was nowhere near the Prague he had left half a century before; nor yet the Central European gem it would become a few short years later when the Czechs realized how much money there was in tourism not hampered by a clumsy and forbidding Iron Curtain.

One scene as they entered the city remains embedded to this day in young Vlad's mind: as they were passing the Russian Orthodox Church of Cyril and Methodius, his father's eyes were suddenly full of tears. This was the place where, in June 1942, the paratroopers who had assassinated Heydrich hid when they were cornered by the Gestapo. Krajina had met them a few days before the assassination. This was where they all died.

And not only the paratroopers. Within days the Orthodox priests of the church were executed along with several thousand Czechs, often picked at random — as was Krajina's brother.

Major changes had taken place in the city since they had left. The Krajinas remembered that to reach the Powder Gate from the river you had to drive along the National Avenue, enter the Street of the 28th of October, then follow Na Příkopě (On the Moat). After that you're practically there. And next to the Powder Gate, everyone knew, was the art deco Hotel Paříž (Paris) where the Krajinas had booked rooms.

That seemed fine. Except that, whereas in 1948 there had been too few cars to bother with, now there was a profusion of tinny Škodas and fibreglass Trabants. The Street of the 28th of October and On the Moat had been changed into pedestrian zones. Because of it, Vlad junior, who was driving, had to find his way through the narrow, curving mediaeval streets of the Old Town. All of this added to the drama of their return. It was a fairy tale come true, an incredibly emotional event which included a reception at the Canadian Embassy.

Hotel Paříž was around the corner from the Czech National Socialists' headquarters, where Krajina had spent countless post-war hours. But this was no time for sightseeing. Upon arrival, the tired Krajinas immediately headed for their rooms and a much needed rest. Earlier, daughter Milena had arranged for a family dinner at the Hotel Paříž dining room. More than thirty relatives from all parts of the country were waiting at its entrance as the family came down after their nap. It was meant as a surprise for Krajina and Marie, but came pretty close to being an all too heady one. Once again surges of emotion raced through the elderly couple. Young Vlad experienced something akin to it, although he saw most of the relatives for the first time, recognizing them from family photographs. It was a memorable evening with even more memorable moments awaiting them.

As the news spread that the Krajinas were back in Prague, scores of visitors started arriving at the hotel. Quickly Vlad and Milena established the strict rule — scrupulously respected by the staff at the hotel's reception — that each afternoon there would be a rest period for their parents. No exceptions allowed.

Some frightening moments came despite the rule. With all the excitement, Marie's arrhythmia problems returned in full force, and one night she even suffered a heart attack. She was taken to a hospital and received excellent care. The attack was a mild one and she was released the next morning. When Milena came to pick her up, she brought a bottle of expensive liquor for the caring hospital staff but it was refused along with any payment. "After all, we are all Czechs," was their simple explanation.

The Czech National Socialist Congress was a bit of an anticlimax.

While Marie rested at home, Krajina delivered his speech, which was unusually diplomatic, perhaps due to his long absence. It was certainly much more conciliatory than the belligerent tone adopted by most of the other speakers. After it was over, the venerable erstwhile general secretary took his seat in the front row, smiling benignly and occasionally waving to old stalwarts.

Milena claims that the absence of his hearing aid came in handy here. He would not have smiled nearly as benignly, and he would not have been nearly as relaxed, had he heard what was being said from the lectern. Old party officials who had happily collaborated with the Communists for years and new ones who had become democratic devotees only during the past four months spouted nonsense. Some insisted on dusting off long forgotten and often doubtful glories. Others interspersed it all with wild predictions about the bright future of the party, which would later be classified as outright idiocies.

As a side note, the nationwide elections came two months later, long after the Krajinas had returned to Canada. The Czech National Socialists finished seventh with 2.75% of the vote, nowhere near the 5% needed to enter the parliament. The collaborating past of the Czech Socialists (as the Communists had renamed them) was not so easily forgotten. Under inept and corrupt leadership, the party had steadily withered away during the succeeding years.

An invitation came from the Castle high above Prague, the seat of former Bohemian kings and now that of the head of state, President Václav Havel. This was still the early part of Havel's term in office, when he had to discard his baggy sweaters and jeans and hurriedly have suits made. It was also when his newly appointed staff, largely assembled from former dissidents, experimented with scooters as a mode of transportation through the long corridors. And when rock musicians were received at the Castle with almost the same frequency as foreign ambassadors and heads of state.

The reception salon was decorated in typical old regime style: squareish and hideously massive armchairs dominated the scene. And yet, despite the forbidding furniture, the atmosphere was incredibly warm. Havel was well aware of the injustice of the former regime toward these national heroes, and he showed his appreciation to the legendary Krajinas.

Marie, upon seeing the president enter room, commented *sotto voce* to her son: *To jsem nevěděla, že on je tak malý pivo!* (I had no idea that he was such a shortie!) In Czech the expression has a somewhat more endearing meaning: *malý pivo* literally means a small beer — something that women order when they don't want to offend the host and at the same time retain their ladylike standing.

When Havel asked what he could do for him, Krajina mentioned that it would be good if Czechoslovakia would bring back the Czech military and underground heroes who had died in exile so that they could be buried in their native land. In his pixieish and somewhat irreverent way, Havel then commented that it could be done and that perhaps the Czech travel agency Čedok could be entrusted with the task. It may have been a good thing that Krajina's hearing aid was still in Vancouver.

In return, Krajina asked what he could do for the president. Havel thought for a moment, then suggested he would like to open the Castle's many terraced lower gardens to the public — something the Communists didn't do — and he would appreciate advice on what should be

Meeting with President Václav Havel at the Prague Castle, 1990.

planted there. To which Krajina smiled, then politely replied that this was a job more for a landscaper than a botanist.

But then the mood changed. The journalists left and Havel suddenly asked if Krajina was a Canadian citizen. When he heard the affirmative answer, he thought for a moment, then quickly had the news people called back. "It was amazing," Vlad remembered later, "because — well, you know Havel — it seemed very spontaneous, but he also thinks before he says anything, and there's usually a pause so that you know an important thing is coming." The president announced Krajina would be awarded the White Lion, the highest Czech decoration, originally intended for foreigners. The Krajinas were invited two days later for the awarding ceremony.

After the meeting with Havel, the family adjourned to the nearby historical *Vikárka* restaurant for lunch. When they had finished the soup, the door to the restaurant opened and in walked the president with his staff, now dressed in jeans and bulky sweaters once more. Krajina mused that fresh winds were blowing through the Castle. Neither the first President Masaryk, from whom he had received a gold watch, nor his successor Beneš, who had decorated him shortly after the war, would have been likely ever to don such attire. But on the whole he enjoyed seeing the unpretentious informality.

Milena remembers that there was no room for her in the car after lunch, and she decided to walk back down into town from the Castle: "It was my first private time since we arrived in Prague and I must have cried all the way. It was all so overwhelming to be in my native town again and to be present when my father was accorded such an honour."

The Order of the White Lion was the only decoration whose origin dated to pre-Communist times, and while it had been awarded to outright scoundrels during the Communist era, the recipients had earlier included Field Marshal Montgomery and General Eisenhower. In that sense then it was a wise decision, symbolically binding Krajina to the pre-Communist era through the decoration. There was, however, one problem: the current version of the decoration had a red star on it.

It was a good thing that there was a two-day leeway between the announcement and the actual presentation. In that time an ardent if not particularly skillful craftsman filed the star away, although traces of the

President Václav Havel presenting the Order of the White Lion
to Krajina at the Prague Castle, 1990.

A toast to the new Czechoslovakia with President Václav Havel at the
Prague Castle after receiving the Order of the White Lion in 1990.

red from the star remained. But, as someone commented, this was also symbolic of the country as a whole.

The actual White Lion ceremony was followed by the laying of a wreath at the statue of the Czech patron saint Wenceslas on the square named after him. The occasion demanded that the wide tricolour with the White Lion on it be worn, and it took several people and a mammoth safety pin to get the bulky contraption over Krajina's head and in place. Still, it was a momentous occasion for everyone who saw it.

During the last part of the sixteen-day visit, the Krajinas drove to Moravia — to Slavice where Krajina was born, and also to Třebíč, where he had moved when he was twelve. It was in Třebíč that he had met Marie.

They arrived in Slavice on a sunny and fairly warm day. Krajina stepped out of the car and smelled the fragrance of the awakening forest, then went to see the school building where he was born. The mayor of the town was waiting there, presenting him first with the traditional bread and salt, and then minutes later with an honorary citizenship of the town.

At nearby Třebíč, there was a public meeting in the building which until recently had been the Communist headquarters. Krajina gave a short speech, and again it was considered a godsend by the family that he was still missing his hearing aid. Evidently one of the unreconstructed local comrades had come expressly to embarrass him by bringing up the many-times discredited chestnut of his supposed wartime collaboration with the Germans.

The last surviving post-war National Socialist deputy, Josef Lesák, a one-time colleague of Krajina's, who had spent many years in a Communist jail, fielded the question, pointing out that, at Krajina's request immediately after the war, an impartial parliamentary commission had been appointed to deal with the accusation. He had been cleared not only by that commission but also by British House of Lords.

Upon returning to Hotel Paříž in Prague, they found a package there from Krajina's daughter-in-law. It contained the forgotten hearing aid — without which his visit had been made so much more enjoyable.

There was one more memorable event. On their night before last in

Czechoslovakia, the four had been invited to the National Theatre by a man named Simon for a performance of his ballet *Jennifer*. The worried Vlad told his father that Marie was in bad shape and that both of them should stay home. It was obvious that his parents were nearing the end of their strength. Too much had been packed into the last two weeks.

As the overture began, Vlad happened to look back and saw his parents quietly entering, taking their seats a few rows behind. They were not going to miss the performance. And before the curtain went up, Mr. Simon stepped out front to tell everyone that in the audience tonight was one of the great Czechoslovak heroes, Vladimir Krajina.

Just before the end of the performance Vlad glanced back and saw that his father's seat was empty. The curtain came down and Simon once more came out in front, this time accompanied by Krajina. When the audience quieted down, Krajina stepped forward and said simply how much he appreciated the author's welcome. And while he allowed that he did help to free the country from the Nazis, he would like to thank all the students who had helped to free it from the Communists. The previous November, only a few blocks away from the theatre, a squad of policemen had brutally dispersed a student demonstration, thereby precipitating the Velvet Revolution.

"It brought the house down," remembers Vlad. "The audience was full of students, and all these kids leapt up to give him a thunderous standing ovation. It was clear, simple and powerful."

Krajina came back to the theater the next evening, this time without Marie, to see Dvořák's opera *Rusalka*. With his hearing aid now firmly in place, he enjoyed it immensely, but the following morning he turned to Vlad to say, "I've had enough. Let's go home."

20

Closing Down

THE RETURN TO Czechoslovakia in effect marked the end of Vladimir Krajina's active involvement in life. There followed a year during which Marie's health steadily deteriorated, and on June 1, 1991, she breathed her last. For Krajina, there was no reason for his own existence after her death. To add to this feeling, a couple of nasty falls now interfered with his walking. Because the house on Chancellor Boulevard held so many memories, Milena and Vlad junior had promised their mother before she died that they would keep Krajina there as long as possible.

They kept their promise, although towards the end Krajina hardly knew where he was anymore. He seldom spoke and when he did his dementia often took over. While earlier he simply stated that after Marie's death he really had nothing more to live for, now he would ask, "Why did she do this to me?" Seeing that he wasn't grasping reality, his children tried to take him for short trips. Vlad recalled how they "tried to

Krajina with his great-grandson, Emil, 1990.

take him places so he wouldn't be living inside his head all the time, but after a few times he'd say: 'I am going to come with you for lunch, but I don't much feel like it — I'm only doing it for you.' So we knew it wasn't working and stopped asking him."

On Christmas morning in 1991 several grandchildren came over and, with Krajina in his wheelchair, there was an enjoyable outing to Vancouver's scenic Jericho Beach. In the days following, however, Milena could see her father deteriorating steadily. He was diagnosed with

Parkinson's disease, and frequent depression fits made his situation worse. Seeing the old agile warrior this way was sad. It was also hard to find people to care for him.

Then, in the spring of 1993, Krajina fell ill with pneumonia and had to be taken to the hospital. He now no longer uttered a word. Milena came to see him every day, fed him lunch and read to him from Karel Čapek's books. It was Čapek who gave the English language the word *robot,* and Krajina used to love his work, but now it was doubtful that he knew what was being read anymore. Vlad came whenever he could.

Milena had planned a European trip that spring and consulted with the doctors. They advised her not to alter her plans: death was not imminent, and this condition could last for months. Milena and her husband departed. A few days later Krajina contracted a urinary infection which, in his weakened state, proved fatal. He died on June 1, 1993 — two years to the day of his beloved Marie's date of death.

The interring of his ashes at Prague's Vyšehrad cemetery came a few weeks later, with his old Resistance friend, Count Kolowrat-Krakovský, rising from his hospital bed, and having his cracked ribs bound for the occasion, so he could officiate at the ceremony. To everyone's shock he started to berate those present for their supposed lack of stamina. Soon, however, the Count settled into a more mellow tone, suggesting that with Krajina's demise an important part of Czech history was being closed.

Perhaps even more poignant was the ceremony around the unveiling of the gigantic Krajina memorial on the front of one of the botanical buildings of Charles University in Prague. It took place in October 2002. The Canadian ambassador Margaret Huber (who came in shockingly short pink pants), attended, as well as the eloquent Czech minister of the environment, Libor Ambrožek. It was Ambrožek who said:

> Madame ambassador mentioned that the Czechs take care of their environment beautifully. I should like to express my conviction that the work of professor Krajina would contribute to making that statement a statement of truth. When in 1990 I was deciding whether I should enter public life, I had before my eyes the legacy of Professor Krajina. It was the legacy of a man who did not shut himself off into

A commemorative plaque for V.J. Krajina placed on the façade
of the Department of Botany of Charles University, Prague. It reads
"Botanist, Politician, National Hero."

the chamber of scientific research. When it became necessary he entered an entirely different sphere — even though his life was directly
threatened by it. The present times are not as critical as our lives are
not directly threatened, but it would still be highly useful if members
of the academic community and graduates of Charles University did
not forget this. It is still very necessary that they do not remain faith-
ful to their scientific research only, but enter the public sphere as
well, attempting to change the world around us.

In Canada the memory of Vladimir Krajina is neither quite as vivid
nor as accurate. Despite being told of its shortcomings several times, the
website of the University of British Columbia gives the incorrect date of
his arrival in Vancouver, then proceeds to describe him as "the former
Secretary of State in the post-WWII government of Czechoslovakia."
Although Czechoslovakia and the present Czech Republic occasionally
had such a position, it is considerably lower than the American equivalent, and Krajina had never held it. It also incorrectly identifies him as
"a former Rector of Charles University in Prague."

Epilogue

IN A WAY, Vladimir Krajina's survival until 1993 constitutes one of the ironies of the 20th century. By all logic he should have been executed during the period of martial law in 1942, or killed by a Gestapo bullet a few months later while zigzagging through the potato field in a region called the Czech Paradise. There a Gestapo man missed his head by something like a centimetre. Or he should have died a few days later when he was finally captured by the Germans and took poison. He narrowly escaped execution at the Terezín concentration camp during a mass slaughter early in May 1945. He could have been assassinated by the Stalinists, during the immediate post-war period when he constituted such a gigantic thorn in their side, or he could have been executed in jail immediately after the Communist takeover in February 1948. Or he could have been shot while attempting to cross the border to freedom a few days later — many others were.

On all of these occasions his death would have made sad sense.

None of it happened. He died in his beloved Vancouver at the blessed age of eighty-eight. It brings to mind an expression coined by the American broadcaster Tom Brokaw. He described the Americans who grew up during the Depression and served in World War II as the Greatest Generation.

Rightly so. They were the ones who served in the greatest war in the history of humankind and won it. In the U.S. the Greatest Generation included such diverse types as John F. Kennedy and Hollywood's Clark Gable. Also Charles M. Schulz, the creator of *Peanuts*. They all saw combat and thereby contributed to the final victory in World War II at sea, in the air and on the ground.

The Canadians too, found their heroes in that generation, among them the handsome but deadly sniper Sgt. H.A. Marshall, the famed writer Farley Mowat or the air ace George "Buzz" Beurling.

And there were members of it on the European continent as well, one of them being Vladimir Krajina. After the war the Greatest Generation in Communist-dominated Central and Eastern Europe was faced with a burden unknown to those members of it returning to Canada and the U.S. On this continent they returned to their homes undisturbed by battles and bombs, to democracies in many ways strengthened by the sacrifices of the war.

In Europe Krajina and others were soon faced with a terrible new choice: either accept totalitarian Communism imposed by a regime headed by an even greater murderer than Hitler, or return to clandestine opposition.

The third alternative was escape. Vladimir Krajina, father of a three-month-old son, a teenage daughter and the husband of a concentration camp veteran in precarious health, chose this way out. Granted that to a man with Krajina's intelligence and practical savvy it couldn't have seemed like much of a choice. He was one of the first of the prominent Czech democratic leaders to cross the border to safety, making sure that his family would soon follow.

We are sometimes prone to envy the Greatest Generation in all parts of the world for the way they dealt with their challenges, for their readiness to risk their lives for what they believed to be right. But we may be a bit unfair to ourselves here. Living in these turbulent times where true national heroes are rare and moral paradigms even rarer, where wars are undeclared, threats undefined and postmodern ideas on morality readily accepted, is not always easy. A few decades ago it may have been somewhat simpler to decide what was right.

Perhaps. That, however, does not reduce Krajina's and others' contribution to the successful ending of the preceding century. Nazism and Japanese militarism were defeated. The very cost of the defeat proved that this would be the last world war ever fought. European Communism eventually collapsed under the weight of its own problems. Krajina and his Greatest Generation played an active part crushing the former, while their moral power was largely responsible in pointing out the fatal weaknesses of the latter. In short, they were instrumental in bringing the twentieth century to a successful close.

Still, the gnawing question should remain in our minds: Given the same set of circumstances and moral challenges would we behave the way Krajina did — as did so many members of his Greatest Generation?

Would we make those highly dangerous yet supremely right decisions?

Select Bibliography

INTERVIEWS:

Krajina-Janda, Milena
Krajina, Dr. Vladimir Jr.
Klinka, Dr. Karel
Moore, Dr. Patrick
Taylor, Dr. Iain

BOOKS:

Bell, Ken. *Not in Vain*. Toronto: University of Toronto Press, 1973.

Brandes, Detlef. *Češi pod německým protektorátem*. Prague: Proster, 1999.

Čvančara, Jaroslav. *Někomu život, někomu smrt, 1939–1941*. Prague: Laguna, 2002.

Čvančara, Jaroslav. *Někomu život, někomu smrt, 1941–1943*. Prague: Laguna, 1997.

Davis, Chuck. *Vancouver Then and Now.* Ottawa: Magic Light Publishing, 2001.

Dějiny Československa v Datech. Prague: Svoboda, 1968.

Drábek, Jaroslav. *Z časů dobrých i zlých.* Prague: Naše vojsko, 1992.

Drtina, Prokop. *Československo můj osud.* Prague: Melantrich, 1991.

Feierabend, Ladislav K. *Ve vládách druhé republiky.* New York: Universum Press, 1961.

Krajina, Vladimír. *Vysoká hra, Vzpomínky.* Prague: Nakladatelství Eva, 1994.

Machotka, Otakar, ed. *Pražské povstání 1945.* Washington D.C.: Rada Svobodného Československa, 1965.

Moore, Patrick. *Trees are the Answer.* Vancouver: Beatty Street Publishing, 2010.

Tichý, Antonín. *Nás živé nedostanou.* Liberec: Edice Lupa, 1968.

Tomášek, Kvaček. *Causa Emil Hácha.* Prague: Themis, 1995.

About the Author

Jan Drabek, whose family has been friends with the Krajinas over many decades, published his first book in 1973. There have been 18 books since, both fiction and non-fiction, published in English and Czech, as Drabek writes in both languages. He is a former president of the Federation of B.C. Writers and former member of the governing council of the Writers' Union of Canada. Drabek has taught high school in Vancouver and served as the Czech ambassador in Kenya and Albania. He now lives with his wife Joan in Vancouver's Yaletown.

Index

Citations of photographs are in bold

Marquis Book Printing Inc.

Québec, Canada
2012